D0409846

A PARENTS' SURVIVAL GUIDE

By the same author

fiction
The Man for the Job

A Parents' Survival Guide

LAURIE GRAHAM

Chatto & Windus

LONDON

Published in 1986 by
Chatto & Windus Ltd
30 Bedford Square
London WC1B 3RP

Fourth Impression 1987

British Library Cataloguing in Publication Data
Graham, Laurie
    A parents' survival guide.
    1. Parenthood
    I. Title
    306.8'74   HQ755.8

ISBN 0—7011—3129—2

Typeset at The Spartan Press Ltd
Lymington, Hants
Printed in Great Britain by
Redwood Burn Ltd,
Trowbridge, Wiltshire

Contents

To Isabel, Alastair, Fiona and Sinead
and to David

Introduction

Some years ago, while I waited for our first child to be born I read a book about parenthood. When I'd finished it, I went on and read about twenty more, and, by the time I was through, what I didn't know about children was not worth the mention. Then we became parents.

Over the next five years four children dropped in on us and liked us enough to stay. We didn't see much of life for a time. When we managed to peer over the top of the laundry basket, everything was hidden by the fog of exhaustion, and we didn't have time to consider what the books had told us, and whether they had been right.

Later the fog lifted. That was when I started to think about all those books.

The first thing I thought was that not a single one of them had told me what being a parent would really be like. And the next thing I thought was that it was time someone wrote a book that would. That was the moment of conception.

Cautious to a fault, I went down to the library to check. I have been losing my grip lately. Forgetting my own telephone number. Locking myself out a good deal. It was possible that I was not remembering right. Perhaps those books *had* spelled it out to anyone with wit enough to read it. I took the most promising-looking book of the shelf and let it fall open at random. I got a page on Masturbation. Bad luck you might say. I flipped the page over. Micturition. My doubts disappeared. I put that book back on the library shelf and went home to my typewriter.

This book is about how parenthood feels. It has no graphs or schedules because they wouldn't help. Without so much as a bar chart I have tried to relate how being the parent of young children is much worse, and at the same time much better, than anything written by an expert could ever convey. In parts the story is so grim that it may come to a final resting place next to the Horror Fiction, but it is a work based on fact. If the children in this book are more gross and their parents more feeble than you would have hoped, it does not mean they are not real.

Virtually everything I describe I have experienced, personally and intimately. The rest is from other reliable sources. Only the names of the hamsters have been changed, to protect the innocent.

I will admit finally to a few gaps. I have not been able to deal with au pairs or stay-at-home fathers, because they are outside the experience of anyone I would trust to tell me the absolute truth. And I have not as yet lived with in-house teenagers. I have observed other people's, as closely as the smell of Dayglo Hair Gel would allow, and I have reported my findings, but in this book the teenagers are not my own. That will be another story, to be written some other day.

Ten Useful Things for a Parent to know

Who holds the record for the highest number of goals scored for England?

The name of the most poisonous snake in the world.

The phone number of a naturalist who will personally vouch for this snake not being found inside children's Wellingtons in Britain.

How to make a scale model of the solar system with ordinary household equipment.

The name of a shop where they sell scale models of the solar system late at night.

How to push a swing and read *The Bleeding Heart* at the same time.

What God looks like.

Whether the Queen is allowed to eat sweets before dinner.

That the answer to 'Are you making a mess in there, Stephen?' is always 'Yes.'

That the answer to 'Are you going to get down off there, Natasha?' is always 'No.'

Ten Useful Things for a Parent to have

A vasectomy

A big stick

A mop and bucket

A pair of toe-tector boots

Shares in Andrex

Inner serenity

A reel of double-sided sticky tape

Somewhere safe to keep it

A loyal family retainer called Nanny

The constitution of an ox

1 *Baby Rules*

Before we go any further – for those of you for whom it's not too late – are you quite sure you know what you're doing? Do you really want to have children? Or are you faking it? Might you not be happier with a timeshare apartment in the Algarve and a cupboard full of handmade shoes?

Let me tell you what's bothering me. There are lots of dumb reasons for having children. You might be thinking of it because your mother is sitting, moist-eyed, with idle knitting pins. You might be doing it out of providence, to fill the years ahead with purpose – acne and arguments and anorexia stored up in Kilner jars as insurance against lonely old age. Or dumbest of all, you might want to prove to the world that parenthood is as easy as falling off a log. Don't do it. Legions have gone before you, equipped with carrycots and optimism, prepared to show that a few kids needn't change anyone's lifestyle, and that one small baby need not deprive anyone of night life, good looks or an Ideal Home. They all finished up with Farex on their trousers.

Babies change everything. I don't care how smart you are. They are smarter. They are also relentless. An arrangement of mouth, bottom and terry towelling that runs away with the years and gives you nothing in return but indiscriminate, unconditional love. Are you still sure?

Then you must consider the details. Like how many, and when. And who's going to look after them. Are you going to be contented with A Child or go for bust and have Children? If you decide that one is enough, you will have what is known in the business as An Only Child. And he has a folklore all of his own.

Did you know, for instance, that the Only Child is precocious, passive, introspective, selfish and socially inept? Haven't you heard

that they grow into insufferable egotists and unaccountable odd-balls? Think back to your school days. Think of the ones who had calfskin attaché cases when everyone else had duffle bags, and the ones who weren't allowed to play in the street because they might have scuffed their shoes or got murdered. Weren't they all Only Children? *Not necessarily*.

As a mother of zillions I must speak up for the Only Child. I was one, am one myself. So are lots of my dearest friends, and a kinder, more lovable bunch a girl couldn't ask for. If their lack of brothers and sisters shows at all, it is in the importance they attach to relationships beyond their immediate family. They hardly ever wish things had been different. They've seen how shabbily brothers and sisters can treat one another.

Don't let anyone put you off having just one child. Provided he's not wrapped in mothballs, he's likely to grow into a perfectly decent sort, and when they've carted you and your photograph albums off to the Twilight Home, at least he won't refuse to come and visit you because he's not speaking to his sister and his brother's wife isn't speaking to anyone.

He'll be cheaper, quieter and faster to mature. He'll become accustomed at an early age to adult conversation and solitude and, if you are the sort of people who won't be able to resist pandering to his every whim, it will be very much easier to do it for one than it will to do it for lots.

Of course, the best laid plans can go wrong. You may intend to have one and end up with more.

Two at a time is called twins, more than two is called a nightmare. If anything like this happens to you you're not going to find a lot of time for reading, so I'll keep this short and to the point.

When it first happens people will be jolly nice about it. They'll rush around borrowing extra high chairs from nodding acquaintances and keep telling you to go and put your feet up for an hour. For about six weeks you will nearly drown in the milk of human kindness, and then suddenly everyone will disappear. The novelty of your conveyor belt existence will have worn off, and you will be left alone with the massed voices of hunger, grizzle and shitty despair.

No one will care that you haven't been able to get out of your housecoat all week. Your house will be littered with mugs of cold coffee and lists of things you're going to do some day; and from time to time a grey, unshaven wreck will shuffle by, to knock over one of those cold coffees and demand that most basic of conjugal privileges, a blazing row.

When you eventually find the time to zip up your slacks and hit the road, total strangers will stop you everywhere you go to tell you what a perfect picture your little family makes, and how they would have loved to have had triplets themselves. Here is what you should do. Put the three-seater buggy firmly in their hands, and offer to send the rest of the luggage on later. They will then laugh nervously, and tell you you can't mean it. Don't be put off by this fickle change of tune. Give them your address and tell them you have sixty little nails to trim on bath night and are not too proud to accept the help of someone who always wanted triplets.

If you've got more than three, people will talk not so much *to* you as *about* you. They'll go into huddles in Boots to give each other the lowdown on how much *Woman's Own* paid for your story, and how many cartons of babycare freebies you've got stashed in your garage. 'Of course,' they'll say tartly, 'they've made an absolute mint out of those quads.'

On the positive side of multiple parenthood, you will have the bonus of instant family chumminess. And later you will find that you have new strengths that come of surviving Trial by Ordeal. And, if ever you feel inclined to look for paid work, you'll find the world is crying out for man-managers of your calibre. You'll be pretty hot at juggling as well.

I'll leave it there. In the two minutes it's taken you to read that, at least one of your babies must be halfway up the stairs with her brother in her mouth and you'll need to be getting on. Just remember that there are lots of us out here willing you to survive. We'll see you in about five years' time.

We boring types who pod out one at a time have to decide for ourselves the size of our folly. You may be adding a thing or two, a wing or two. It comes down to this. How tired and poor are you prepared to be, and for how long? If you have your children close together, the exhaustion will be extreme but it will be over faster, leaving you a clear run of about twenty years for wild parties, adult movies and still being awake for *News at Ten*, before they start lumbering you with the grandchildren and it starts all over again. If you space them wider, your body will have time to recover from each assault, and then, just as it's nodded off into normality you'll spring it the ugly surprise of another stint on the night shift. It depends which you're better at, sprints or hurdles.

Three years is a favourite gap. I shall never understand why. A three year old is a loathsome thing. Ideally it should be put in a deep freeze until it is of school age. If you introduce it to a new brother or sister, it will aspire at once to new heights of loathsomeness. It will help you by talcum powdering the whole house. It will demand breast milk with menaces and, when you offer it your spare breast, it will run away and play its xylophone all afternoon. And it will completely forget that it ever knew what a potty was for.

Younger than three they are too ga-ga to notice that you've slipped another one in. Later on they may ask but you can just say, 'Abigail? She's your sister. She's been here for years.'

From about five onwards children can be very nice about newcomers. They show genuine affection and pride where the baby is concerned, are nearly always willing to humour anyone who is hot and bored with being six months old, and they can be very helpful about fetching and carrying for you.

Girls are especially good at this age. With boys it comes later. If you're planning on having a teenager and a baby in the same family, let the teenager be a boy. Teenage boys are gentle, solicitous and generally wonderful about pregnancy and babies. Don't be surprised if your house is suddenly full of lurking lads with lovely bodies and horrible complexions. These are your son's friends and they are willing to help. Let them. They can make you a cup of tea, or allow your Golden Retriever to take them for a walk, and you can reward them with the Dial-a-Pizza of their choice.

If your teenager is a girl it will be a very different story. She'll start complaining as soon as she knows you're pregnant, and she won't let up. About how she can never hold her head up again because it's so gross, so embarrassing. She'll be worried about the baby waking her because she'll be at an age when she really needs her sleep, what with CSEs and having to stay up till all hours piercing each other's ears and pitying people who are over twenty. And you needn't think she's stopping in to babysit for you, because she's not. She has become a hunter of men. Well, not strictly men. Rather, a slightly sweatier, more knowing version of the ones who like holding babies and chatting to lactating old ladies. Like all predators, she doesn't have a lot of time for hanging around. A snatched three hours in the bathroom, re-applying the Pan-Stik and she'll need to be back out there on Mean Street, sniffing for trouser and taking no prisoners.

Probably the best thing is not to tell her at all. She won't notice the pregnancy because she thinks you're obscenely fat anyway. If she notices anything after the birth, just tell her it's something you've borrowed for a few days. No need to burden her with the details. By the time you get to the word 'borrowed', she will have switched on her Walkman.

As for numbers, the more you have, the higher your running costs, but not proportionately so. Things get handed on and made over, and, somehow, the bigger the family, the more cheerful everyone is about being scruffy. And the more of you there are to huddle together on a bleak winter's night, the less you'll spend on coal. There's no escaping the fact that eight people eat more than four people, but they do not necessarily eat twice as much, and there is a lot less waste.

The advantage of the larger family is that it is far less labour-intensive. Parents of one or two children always seem to work a lot harder to achieve the same results. They have no sooner settled themselves with the *News of the World* and a Duncan's Walnut Whip than there is a child standing before them with Snakes and Ladders and a look of wistful loneliness. Where there are two children and two parents there is an unspoken assumption that you will pair off, either in the modern fashion with the sexes crossed, or in traditional style, with the women icing biscuits and the men grouting tiles.

In a large family you get a much better mix. There's always someone around to play Ludo or have a quarrel with you, and everyone can have a turn at being a good sport, or an unapproachable grouch.

Nowadays four is considered a large family, but three is not. More than four is reckoned to be a symptom of Catholicism, insanity, or an ancient and aristocratic pedigree. Unlike the newly rich, who settle for two children and a well-maintained suntan, old money likes to have lots of children. That way they get plenty of wear and tear out of everything they buy, they have a better chance of keeping warm when the wind whistles through the east wing, and they are never short of good homes for all those silver spoons and ugly sideboards they are honoured to own.

You may have some limited control over how many children and their age differences, but you are stuck with who they are and what they think of one another. There is likely to be one relationship that grates. You can't do anything about it except hope for improvement or emigration when they get to adulthood. Some brothers and sisters will never like one another. But, in general, the question of who hates whom will go in phases.

Nine year old boys for instance, are not very highly rated by thirteen year old girls. But when that thirteen year old was nine and her brother was five, there's every chance that they were the best of friends. The scene shifts endlessly, so no problem need be with you for long. Just remember that the more biddable the girl when she is young, the louder the hysterics when she grows up; that cockiness in the pre-pubescent boy gives way eventually to introspection and stubble on the chin; and that in each generation, every family worth its salt throws up one misanthropic crab. The fact that yours has freckles and a pony tail does not mean that the rest of the world is wrong and she is right.

Some children get out of bed the wrong side the very first day, and that's the way they stay. If by a cruel trick of genetics you find yourself with more than one of these characters in your family, you should insist that they bunk down in the same room, and get yourself the best earplugs money can buy.

When you've got them, who is going to look after them? Will one of you stay home, for a year or two, or ten? Or will you pay someone a lot of money to bring them up for you? And, if you're united in the view that one of you should stick around for the formative years, who is it going to be?

Whichever of you it is, you're not going to be doing it for ever. If you're a man you probably already have a very clear idea of how long you're going to do it for and what you're going to do afterwards. If you're a woman your plans are likely to be much more vague. Get the youngest one settled in school and then see about doing something? Something different as like as not because you never felt really *galvanised* by food technology, and you'd actually quite like to study Arabic. Some day.

There are things you should know about Life After Small Children. The first is this. If there's even the remotest chance that you'll want to take a break and then go back to the work you did before, *keep your hand in*. Do a bit of part time, put yourself about, and copy the boys, by hanging on to every slightly useful contact you ever make. If you don't, round about your thirty-second birthday you will start to become invisible, and by thirty-five there will be less left of you than there was of the Cheshire Cat. I don't care how marvellous everyone said you were in 1979.

Of course you might not want to go back. You might want a complete change. To retrain. Or set up your own business. The second thing you should know is this: *beware of pretending*. Just as reading articles in *Good Housekeeping* on quick, delicious meals for working mothers is not the same as being a working mother and coming home to a tin of cornflour and a bag of frozen peas, so having a go at a few pressed flower pictures is not the same as opening your own craft shop.

After years of wiping a nose as you scramble the eggs as you answer the telephone and say No to the Avon lady through the window, it is difficult to settle to sustained concentration on one thing. And that's what you will have to do if you're going to study or create or innovate. You will have to become selfish, demanding, and at times, completely unavailable. And that's not very nice, is it?

If you are going to be the one who goes out every morning and comes home most evenings, in the eyes of your children you will be a magical figure. They'll look forward to the sound of your key in the door and they'll hug you a lot. A lot more than if you'd been there all afternoon making gingerbread men or upstairs, with your oil paints and a heavy cupboard against your door, shouting, 'I'm not here!'

If you do something interesting, like working in a toy shop, or cutting the hair of someone whose brother used to live next door to Ian Rush, your children will also be very proud and approving. If you're a working father this may give you no more than passing pleasure. But, if you are a working mother, such approval will mean a lot to you. Your children may give it gladly, but the rest of the world will not. School will be politely chilly about it, Granny will be pained to hear that the children's coughs never seem to get any better, and Society will be prepared to blame you for everything, from Junk Food to the Militant Tendency.

The other thing that happens to you when you have children is that you are bound to have more to do with other people's children. A lot of it will be unavoidable. At first there will be the children your family and close friends have produced. Later the circle will widen. There will be neighbours' children, school friends and eventually your own grandchildren. Please remember you are not obliged to like any of them.

If you have no children yourself, other people's babies are not very interesting. If you're busy revising for your Bar finals, or establishing goodwill and a paying clientele for your mobile chiropody service, the number of teeth your nephew can boast will not be as riveting as your sister may suggest it should be.

But, if you have a young family yourself, you'll really be into teeth. And stretch marks. And wipeable surfaces. It can be very cosy, a lot of you with youngsters of about the same age. So much will not need to be explained. The little dollops of used kitchen paper behind the settee. Not being able to use the front door because the pram is in the way. And the way you keep falling asleep in the middle of a sentence.

There will be so much to talk about. Natural childbirth can last a whole dinner party. The man you would have sworn was smarter than Jeffrey Archer will talk foetal monitoring all the way through to the crème brûlée with the man everyone said was funnier than Miles Kington. At times like these it's good to be among friends.

It changes the day one of the juniors takes his first step. The minute he's on the move you will start to discover what a menace children can be, especially when they belong to people you always thought were your friends.

There are two common mistakes. One is to think that because you like the parents you will also like the child. The other is to suppose that you can all carry on the way you used to. Grown-ups together, laughing, arguing, drinking each other's undrinkable wine and hardly being interrupted at all by the chaps in the terry snuggle suits. No one wants to have to stop halfway through every sentence to say, 'Take that out of your mouth, Tobias.' No one wants to leave their chilli to go cold while they step outside to make Prudence see reason.

The sad truth is that small, mobile children and the normal social life of a friendly adult are incompatible. You ask old friends round for a game of Mah Jong and a Peking Garden Dinner for Six, and what happens? They bring Jake with them. He pulls all the books off your shelves and they are so busy telling you about their Bargain Break Weekend in Amsterdam that they don't even notice. They bring along a jaunty collapsible cot, and he refuses to collapse in it. A stripy leg keeps appearing over the side, and he will still be up at midnight, dribbling all over the prawn crackers. Before the sun rises, you will hate him. You have known his parents for years. You would have staked your life on their knowing how to handle Jake. And now here he is, swinging from your Swiss cheese plant and calling you Nunkie.

What do you do? Put up with it in the name of friendship and then swear a lot after they've gone home? Rip them out of your address book? Or take them to one side and tell them, 'Tim, Patsie, we go back a long way so we know you'll thank us for telling you that Becky is not welcome to sit on her potty during our poker games. We'll call you again when she's left home.'

Brave words! Are you really up to that sort of performance? I'm not. I love my friends and I want to keep them.

As their children get older and your children get older, the friendship will be put well and truly to the test. One of theirs will fight with one of yours and you will be asked to act as referee. Each will say the other started it, cross their hearts and hope to die, and you'll end up blaming your own kid for everything that's gone wrong that day, from the breakdown in East–West relations to the fact that the fire has gone out. After your friends have gone, you can apologise until you're blue in the face, but your child will have learned something he will never forget. That visiting children get away with daylight robbery. And that blood is not necessarily thicker than water.

Your children will get to know which visitors to dread. I think it helps to be honest. Tell them you know what they go through. A word or two about stiff upper lips. It won't hurt them. Wherever they go in life there's going to be someone waiting to jump on their train set.

Friendship is one thing. Neighbourliness is quite another. If your neighbours have children of an age with your own, you will find that their relationship with one another will be one of extremes. They will either live in each other's houses, swapping their most prized possessions, dressing identically and begging not to be parted even for eight hours of essential sleep; or it will be all-out war: verbal abuse, party invitations rescinded, and footballs not thrown back over the garden fence. Talking of fences, I recommend nothing less than six feet. All the way round.

If war is declared, you'll find girls are worse than boys. Boys have a quick wrestle in the gutter, the winner goes home to crow, the loser goes home for Elastoplast and they're back out there on their pogo sticks by next morning, the very best of friends. Girls go on for weeks. Writing notes. Lobbying for useful support. And watching carefully for that special moment when they know they can negotiate from a position of advantage. It beats me why more of them don't go into politics when they grow up.

As parents, what you are not supposed to do is get involved. This is a modern, middle-class convention. In olden times women were for ever out on their doorsteps exchanging compliments. It was a cheap and wholesome form of entertainment. If you thought your neighbour's child was a venomous, scabby-kneed doughball, you could say so, loud enough for it to be generally broadcast, and not be the least surprised to hear that your own pet lamb was a raggy-arsed thief who probably took after his father if only anyone knew who his father was. Now we are supposed to be above that sort of degrading behaviour. It is considered more fitting to plump the cushions and say pleasantly, 'I expect you'll be friends again soon.' But mark my words. No good ever came out of such repression. Small wonder there's so much psoriasis on these new estates.

Your neighbours may not be your friends. Why should they be? Just because your houses are stuck together is no reason for there to be a deep and meaningful relationship between you. Where I grew up it was absolutely understood that no one had a kind word to say for anyone. If you broke your leg, they fetched your shopping in for you, and if you died, they collected for a wreath, but that was as far as it went. And if there was trouble between children, there was a great putting on of coats over pinnies, and hammering on doors with offers of bodily violence from one absent husband to another.

Other people's children *can* be fascinating. They can make you realise things about your own children, like how nice they are. They can jolt you into asking yourself questions, such as 'Am I turning my children into social pariahs by allowing them to use the word *bum*?' and 'Does my lavatory cleaner *really* get right up under the rim?' Other people's children can give you titillating glimpses of what goes on behind closed doors. Some children look at you in such startled terror when you ask them if they'd like an egg sandwich that you realise no adult has ever spoken to them politely before. Some just run up and down stairs and bang doors a lot, without even seeming to notice you. These are the ones with timid, low-profile parents whose hearing is not what it used to be.

Some will eat nothing but chips. Some have never seen fresh fruit. And some will arrive with their carpet slippers, their own towel and a disposable medicated cover to put over your lavatory seat.

One or two will arrive uninvited. This happens a lot when your child first starts school. He turns up with total strangers who tell you they are allergic to cheap beefburgers. Or three weeks before his birthday you hear that he has personally invited all forty of his classmates to his party. You then have the thankless job of dealing out invitations to the favoured few and dealing with anxious enquiries from the reserve list and their mothers.

The ones you do invite will give you the largest dose of other people's children you are ever likely to have to swallow. Most of them will be there because your child went to their party, duty coming before pleasure even for the very young. One or two will be there because of bribery, string-pulling and spontaneous goodwill. The best ones of all are the accomplished party-goers. They know how to ask for the toilet. They are not shy of any strange adults you may have hanging around, like aunts with teeth that click or grandads that do the Twist. And, when it's time to go home, they know exactly which coat is theirs, and how to line up for a balloon on a string and to say Thankyouforhavingme.

I've met about a dozen children like this in years of looking, and thousands of the other sort.

Like I said, get a six-foot fence.

One of the most glaring design faults in human babies is that they want dinner parties in the middle of the night. You may know a smug, healthy-looking couple who've given a home to a mutant who sleeps round the clock, but life is full of irritations that must be borne. Some people never get greenfly on their roses. Or run out of toilet paper at ten o'clock on a Sunday night. Wherever you go, you'll bump into some clever dick who's got it taped. For the rest of us, the grim truth is that a baby means less sleep. Quite a lot less. Let me spell it out to you. Small babies don't know the difference between day and night. Eventually they learn, but it can be a long hard haul. It can take years.

You probably know this already, but, if you haven't yet had a child, let me tell you another interesting fact. Knowing it is one thing. Believing it is something else. I'll set the scene for you.

Attila is five days old. He weighs seven and a half pounds and is doing fine. You've probably brought him home from St Harpic's, changed his clothes several times because his nappy doesn't fit around his thin legs and he keeps evacuating into his boots and up his vest, and you've finally tucked him up in his very own room, with his very own co-ordinated curtains, wallpaper and duvet cover and, of course, matching eye shades for the rocking horse. You've put out the milk bottles and the cat, held hands several times and said, 'At last, darling, we're a proper family,' and you're ready for eight hours of oblivion. All along the street the lights go out, and you fall asleep. Just as a new phase of your life is about to begin.

The first thing you'll know about it will be that you are awake when you didn't mean to be. Then you'll hear something. Not a full-blooded cry. Just the overture to one. It will sound like a car engine on a cold morning, nearly firing but not quite making it.

You will find yourself lying very still, and holding your breath. You will find yourself believing that it might go away. And you'll probably find yourself lying next to someone who is fast asleep and hasn't heard a thing.

After a while you'll give in and get up. You'll feed him, change his clothes again, feed him a bit more, and, exhausted by all this activity, young Attila, now nearly six days old, will fall asleep. His warm, downy, little head will nestle against your neck. He'll look tiny and vulnerable and smell of baby powder, and, after you've made him snug in his cot, you'll get to thinking that it wasn't so bad after all.

He'll bide his time. He'll listen to you taking off your dressing gown and telling The Hump how many ounces of milk he took. He'll listen for the sound of the springs when you get back into bed and he'll wait until your head has actually touched the pillow. Then he'll open one beady eye, erupt warmly down the leg of his pyjamas and start the cold engine routine all over again.

The next day you'll feel a bit rough, but you'll get by. You'll still be getting the hothouse grape treatment, with afternoon naps, and you will have great reserves of strength. It will be later on that it will really get to you. It can go on for months, and to be woken, suddenly and insistently, every night for a long stretch, is one of the most exquisite forms of torture ever devised.

Firemen aren't expected to be On Watch night after night without a break, for the good reason that it curdles the brain. Firemen have other firemen and they take turns. But most of us have to fly solo. Job-sharing hasn't happened in a big way in this line of work, and anyone else that may be in the house with you has probably got to get up at seven to be a Captain of Industry. So you're on your own. And, while you are providing this 24-hour catering service, things will happen to you. You will become obsessed with sleep. You'll talk to total strangers about how you're not getting it, fantasise about how it used to feel, and, in the fulness of time, be ready to murder for it. You'll walk around in a mist, as though the wick isn't quite dipping in your oil, and, if you go on to have other children in rapid succession, you'll live in an absolute pea-souper for years. If it clears in time for your fortieth birthday, you'll be amazed to find that the world is still turning and there are friends out there smiling and offering you a glass.

At the beginning, the night shift is simple. Tiny babies wake mostly because they need food. He'll want a little at a time, and often. And he'll tire quickly. Books written by experts will tell you to check he's not crying because his nappy needs changing. I never met a baby that bothered to wake up and yell on such a flimsy pretext. A wet nappy is a warm nappy and every baby I ever spoke to rather liked rolling around in it for a while. Hours later, when it's gone stone cold, it will be a different story but, all other things being equal, it will not be the reason he's getting you up. At the beginning it will be food.

Have you heard the one about bathtime and the ten o'clock feed? You'll like this one. It's an old chestnut but you can still find it in earnest books on Mothercraft. It's based on the bottle-fed baby and a deep reverence for the ticking of the clock. It goes something like this. Baby needs a bottle every four hours. This far I'm with them. He needs a bottle at 10 a.m., 2 p.m., 6 p.m., 10 p.m. and 4 a.m. Now they're starting to lose me. But there's more. Knowing all this, Mother can plan her day with military exactitude. Before the 10 a.m. feed she has time to get the nappies on the line and give Attila his daily soaping down in the bath. After his 10 a.m. bottle he'll sleep in his pram until 2.00, giving Mother time to do her housework and prepare lunch. *And*, by obligingly sleeping from 2.30 until 6.00, he will allow her time to listen to *Woman's Hour* and have Father's jam roly poly dished up before he rears his little head and asks for *his* tea. These schedules are written for Toy Town people. If you still have a thing called Wash Day, if people sniff at your kitchen door and say, 'Liver! It must be Wednesday,' you may find a use for this sort of timetable. Otherwise, turn the clock to face the wall and remember that with a baby around times become very – ish.

So a breast-fed baby needs feeding every three hours-ish and a bottle-fed baby every four hours-ish, and in either case the effort of taking the food will drive him back to sleep quickly.

As he gets older, he'll be more interested in the general quality of the 2 a.m. experience. The milk may be delicious and you may be serving it at exactly the right temperature, but it may not be enough. He may sit up and say, 'Bring on the dancing girls. Let the jugglers and the fire-eaters appear.' This is when you realise that he's dragged you from your bed, not because he's hungry, but because he's bored witless by his roommates. The horse never goes any place, the bear in the boots and the dufflecoat has never been heard to speak, and Attila is desperate for a little action. This is really hard to take. You know that out there in Langan's Brasserie the night is young, but this is Bishop's Stortford and you suddenly feel old. Who is this joker who wants to play Pat-a-Cake? Can't he tell the time? And are you the only person left alive in the whole wide world?

Of course not. Think about it. There are thousands of you. Wouldn't it be great if you could all get together? Wouldn't it be marvellous if you could move into a night-shift commune and take a break from playing Happy Families? A sort of refuge where you could stay until your child twigged that there will be no Busby Berkeley spectaculars at dawn. Then you could go home, leaving a place for some other Farex-stained desperado. You'd never run out of people to talk to and you'd get away with things like eating breakfast in the afternoon, and not washing your hair for a fortnight.

Failing this, all you can do is make the inescapable as pleasant as possible for yourself. I use the word inescapable advisedly. There is no way out of it but through it.

You will meet people who say they can cure a baby of waking in the night. They are charlatans. 'Give him a huge meal at bedtime,' they say. So you force-feed him on turbot and mushrooms in a white wine sauce and he stays silent until mid-morning. You are still up all night worrying whether you've damaged him, but he'll be out for the count. A couple of days later you find that to achieve the same effect you're having to supplement this with Stilton, celery and a selection from the pudding trolley, and at the end of a week you've got a three month old the size of a three year old, and he'll still want to get up in the night because he likes your face.

'Try drugging him,' they say. This is immoral. Effective, but highly immoral. I say this from the safe ground occupied by those who no longer have small babies.

'Try a dummy,' they say. A *dummy*? I hear a sharp intake of breath from my mother and yours. Dummies deform the jaw, displace the teeth, and ruin the moral fibre of all concerned. No wonder we lost the Empire. Dummies also silence babies for a while so, if you're desperate, try one. I'm with you all the way. Provided

you don't put anything on it. Like sugar. If you put sugar on it, I wash my hands of you. If you have twins or worse, I'd say a dummy was all that stood between you and insanity.

'He's cold. Try a Mister Snuggly Walk-In Sleep Suit,' they say.

'He's frightened. Try a Mister Cuddly Glow Worm Nite Lite,' they say.

'He's a wicked manipulative demon,' they say. 'Leave him to scream.'

All nonsense. The truth is simple. The rhythm of sleep and wakefulness is something that matures at different times in different people. Like riding a bike or saying No to your mother, you do it when you're ready and not before. It *will* happen to your child, though you may find it hard to believe right now. One morning you'll wake up and something won't feel right. You'll know you have left undone something you ought to have done. You haven't moved all night. And neither has he. Your child has learned about sleep, and now you can carry on with the rest of your life. Congratulations.

But until this happens your nights and days will blend into a milky dusk, and you may as well make it as pleasant as you can.

The best sort of comfort is other human beings. They top anything that comes out of a bottle or a chocolate box, so if you've noticed a light on in the house opposite at four every morning, make a few enquiries. You could end up with a new friend. Or a black eye. In my street, if there was anyone who wasn't asleep at that unnatural hour they never let on, at least not to a wild-eyed woman in a dressing gown and a pair of men's socks. But things may be different round your way. If not, it's back to the chocolate box. Oral comforts are not to be sneered at. Having something good to put in her mouth has helped many a desperate woman through a long night. So, if you have to be up, fill your cup, load your plate and enjoy having time to think. Some of my grandest plans have been laid on the night shift.

The one thing you won't dream of doing is taking the child into bed with you. Will you? It's a practice that's fraught with dangers – like your staying warm and comfortable while Attila does what a lad has to do. Added to which, there's the point about your bed being your territory and your children needing to learn to respect it. We all know what can come of laxness over sleeping arrangements.

I have a lot of experience of beds. Let me help you.

If you are very, very tired and you have a baby who likes to suck his way through the night, keeping him in bed with you can be a very sound move. If you or your partner weighs more than eighteen stone, or one of you habitually goes to bed blind drunk, there *is* a risk of your rolling on the child and suffocating him. Otherwise, there is not. You will develop an instinct that will keep you from disturbing him at all, and, if you have a breastfeeder who's still at it after six months, *he* will learn to crawl from one side to the other and help himself without disturbing *you*. The only pitfall to this

cosy arrangement is not recognising when the time has come for him to go back to his own quarters and be a big boy. There does come a time and, if your son has started getting Brylcreem on your pillow, I'd say you ought to act swiftly.

Don't misunderstand me. I'm not totally opposed to the concept of the Family Bed. I've nothing against them all getting into bed with me on Sunday mornings. Six people eating custard creams can create quite a lot of crumbs, and twelve legs do generate a lot of heat, but it can be a good time to relax, be a family, and discuss who has made that terrible smell.

But nights are different. It's mainly to do with size and fidgetiness. He should be sleeping in his own bed before it gets to the point of you clinging to the edge of the mattress while he impersonates a starfish. You may think that sounds obvious, but you wouldn't believe what some parents will endure.

There are those who insist from the beginning that their child sleeps in his own bed and only sets foot in the master suite if he has a warrant bearing a royal seal, but are prepared to crawl into *his* bed with *him* if he gets troublesome at bedtime. They only intend to do it the once. He grizzles because his Darth Vader slippers are coming to get him, so someone gives in and agrees to play at Sleeping Lions. I guarantee one of two things will happen. Either Daddy falls asleep and the little lad stays wide awake till midnight playing with a bed full of Meccano. Or the ploy works, the child sleeps, the parent slips quietly out of the bed and, just as his hand reaches the dimmer switch, young Genghis wakes up and roars that his parents are cheating on him and that those slippers have *moved*.

I've seen good people keep this sort of thing going for years. I've seen them explain carefully about Mummies and Daddies needing time to themselves and about bodies needing rest. It has never got them anywhere. It seems to me that, if you've reached the stage of having to tiptoe out of his bedroom, he probably isn't susceptible to reasonable argument. He needs telling straight. Here's a suggested script in case you're lost for words. You can, as they say in the magazines, ring the changes with little touches of your own. Say,

'Listen, you little worm. I'm tired. You're tired. Set one foot out of that bed and I'll thump you. Darling.' And then, when he does (and he will), thump him.

Once he's absorbed that simple lesson you can afford to be flexible about beds. I encourage all of my children to sleep around. Packing an overnight bag and going to stay with friends is something even a four year old can do. Like all travel it broadens the experience, narrows the mind and promotes appreciation of the place they call home. By overnighting my children learned a lot. Like how to phone home for a food parcel, and what a hairbrush is really for.

Sleeping out is good, too. A tent in the garden is a good face-saver for an eleven year old who isn't understood, especially if she can't afford the fare to Australia. And within the family I'd always encourage children to be accommodating about where they sleep. That way they can be doubled up to make space for unexpected visitors and they can migrate from one room to another, according to which brother or sister is the flavour of the month. My children play musical beds all the time and, provided none of them tangles with me and my bedclothes, I don't interfere.

But to return to the tinies, who truly can't help the unsocial hours they keep. If this is your first child the secret of sane survival is that it is all a matter of attitude. Don't think of yourself as getting less sleep. Rather think of it as changing your sleep pattern. Because here is the good news. If your baby is up and down all night, there will be times during the day when he will sleep. And when he does, so can you. But, I hear you say, the windows haven't been cleaned for weeks, and I'm renowned for my homemade cakes. My answer to this and any other feeble excuses you may have lined up is this. *Knickers*. Knickers to the windows and knickers to the cakes. Close the curtains so you can't see the sunlight playing on the grime. Put from you all magazines that tell you how to knock up a Crunchy Farmhouse Tuna and Apple Bake in less than half an hour, and, if you really cannot live without cake, put a little business in Mr Kipling's direction, take the phone off the hook and SLEEP.

Five minutes is worth having. Ten minutes is twice as worth while. Don't tell me you feel groggy if you nod off during the day. If you're going without sleep at night, groggy is normal anyway and, though you may feel groggier still when you first wake up, later on you'll feel a lot better. And don't tell me you can only sleep in total darkness in a winceyette nightie. Now is the time to start doing it in a chair with your wellies on. If you have other children this is harder. If they're young, they'll make menacing demands for drinks of orange and *Watch with Mother*, and, if they're at school, you'll be up against the double tyranny of a baby and a school timetable. Attila will howl for food and cabaret just as the clock strikes 8.30 and you need to play Hunt the Plimsoll, and drop off to sleep when it's time to trudge to school and trudge home again with an armful of wet paintings. This is when you see the advantage of having them all under school age together, or waiting until your first child has grown spots and a beard before you risk having the second one.

Just understand this. Juggling with broken nights, the descant recorder as played by a six year old, and the pressing problem of what your ten year old can take for Harvest Festival when you have nothing in your vegetable basket except a headless Sindy doll and a potato that has put down roots, will all take their toll. Your temper will be shorter, your hair will lack bounce, and you will wonder how it feels to have a career in banking and seven hours a night between designer sheets. If you have a large family, by the time you get to your last tour of duty you won't even bother to think about sleep any more. You will do it all the time while appearing to be awake and in control of things, and your child will do it wherever he finds himself in a moment of need. Our youngest child has been found asleep in a laundry basket. She has also been found asleep on the bottom step of the stairs, and on top of a brother who was watching the Late Friday Frightener.

As time passes nighttimes will throw up new challenges. Once your

child has learned to sleep, he'll then learn how to have nightmares. This means that you'll always be on emergency call. If he wakes up wailing and you find he's got a whole train-set in bed with him, he may just be uncomfortable, or he may be anxious because the guard's van has fallen on the floor. You'll know instinctively what to do. I've always found losing my temper helps. Then, when I have brought the child to a closer understanding of my emotional state, I deal with the practicalities. Maybe make up a bed for him in the train-set box.

But it may be that there is no rational solution to a distressed child in the middle of the night. He may be very frightened and, if he is, it's no use trying to jolly him out of it. If you say things like 'How the hell can there be sharks on a parquet floor in Birmingham?' he'll only howl louder. Far better to go along with his story. I've spent many an hour on my knees and naked, rifling under the bunks with a broom handle and yelling, 'Okay, Big Green Bear, your number is up. Get out from under the bed and understand this, no one, *but no one*, eats small boys while I'm around.' Kids find this sort of performance very comforting, especially if they've seen what you can do with a broom handle. And, if you have personal problems with sharks and Big Green Bears, parenthood will be the making of you. The need to be seen as strong and dependable will soon have you on easy terms with spiders, worms and things that go bump in the night.

Then there's the business of bedtimes. There will come a time when your child will not be content with a dry nappy, a nursery rhyme and lights out at seven. He'll have homework to do and friends dropping in for drinks. Too many rules about the hours people keep can lead to head-on collisions.

I've come to the view that when a body gets to be seven or eight he can start to exercise a little self-discipline. Some folks need a lot of sleep, some can get by on next to nothing. If your child can read Willard Price until midnight and still grace the breakfast table with intelligent conversation, why argue? If children are given some control over how late they stay up, they will develop a decent attitude towards going to bed early when they've had an exhausting day. This sounds a bit soft, but don't be nervous. If he stays up late and is unbearable for the rest of the week, he's too young to set his own bedtime. Try him again in a year's time. He has to be grown-up enough to see things both ways. All I insist on is that I can go to bed when I want to. This is vital. I don't care how exciting the snooker promises to be.

And I apply the same rule on those mornings when we're all free to get up when we please. I was brought up on alarm clocks, bacon and eggs and a clean shirt every morning, but, if my children want *Sesame*

Street and a banana for breakfast, I can see no reason to interfere. They know where my door is if they need me. As long as they remember to knock. And as long as they don't necessarily expect me to be civil. Many a visiting child has been struck dumb by the sight of a mother in bed with Jack Kerouac and a pot of tea, when she might be strapped into her pinny, grilling sausages. I would like to think I have shone a light into some dark corner of their minds.

Gradually the night calls upon you will grow fewer. Attila will get old enough to fix himself a sandwich, if he gets hungry after the staff have knocked off, and he'll learn to read a book or make an Airfix model if he's not sleepy. These glorious times will come. Until they do, you should try nothing heroic.

Cut corners. Cat-nap. And listen while I tell you about a couple of little time-savers. First, the Clean Sweep. The principle behind this is that neatly arranged dirt is easier to ignore than clean clutter. You'll need a large plastic sack. With children you nearly always need a large plastic sack. Once a day/week/year, depending on how low you have sunk, drop into it everything you find lying in your path. This transforms a room in minutes and has a useful spin-off. It trains your family out of leaving things in heaps. The agony of having to dive into a sack full of other people's trash to find their own important and precious things helps them to grasp the idea of putting things away as they go. And just one clear table, just one floor you can walk on without breaking your ankle, can do wonders for the spirits after a long hard day trying to stay on top.

The second tip is the Ironing Basket Skim. I'm assuming you've already worked out that you never iron anything you think you can get away without ironing. You're now ready for A-level Avoidance of Ironing. This technique evolved when I noticed that there were always things at the bottom of the basket that never got ironed. They were things that needed major repair work and things that we hated but were too cowardly to throw away. Slowly my life was filling up with trouserless zips and polyester frocks that made my daughter sob piteously. I decided to act. Now, twice a year without fail, I skim off all items that move in and out of the basket at least once a week. They have earned their place in my life and are safe, for the time being. Then I up-end what's left into another of those large plastic sacks and send it to a jumble sale as quickly as possible. Somehow we never miss any of it.

You can extend this principle to any other trouble spots. Is your kitchen cupboard full of damn fool things like angelica and aerosol cans that have lost their nozzles? Well, now you know what to do.

Remember, as well, not to make anything you can reasonably buy, not to buy anything you can do without, and to be careful of the company you keep. Have nothing to do with Supermum and Wonderdad. Steer very clear of people who make patchwork quilts with one hand and choux pastry with the other.

And consider this. At the end of it all you will have acquired a useful new skill. You will have learned how to sleep in a supermarket checkout queue without anyone suspecting a thing.

3 *The Professionals*

In the pre-school years, even if you're lucky enough to have a healthy able-bodied child, you will come face to face with the professional carers. People who have chosen to devote the best years of their lives to the care of children and other minorities. You'll meet midwives, health visitors, doctors and dentists. You need not pull your forelock, throw yourself to the ground, or stand before them in awe-struck silence. They are mostly human beings. You must remember this. They have prejudices, blind spots and bad days. And they are not divine.

Midwives come first, of course. There are two sorts. Hospital midwives should not be confused with the ones who drive nippy little cars full of cottonwool around country lanes. These are a different breed.

In a hospital, scratch a midwife and you'll find a nurse. Her early training will have emphasised the importance of orderliness, cleanliness and emotional detachment. So if she's a bossy and compulsive bed straightener, is it any wonder? And is it surprising that so few nurses transfer successfully to the chaotic warmth of midwifery?

Newborn babies spell ANARCHY, and good midwives don't bother to fight it. They are very special people, skilled, compassionate and full of common sense. If you meet one of these rare creatures, embrace her warmly and buy her a large bottle of Je Reviens.

If, on the other hand, you find yourself under the eagle eye of a midwife who is obsessed with disinfectant and the regularity of your bowel movements, you should seriously consider applying for early parole. The most favourable consideration is given to applicants who are trouble-makers and to those who are in fine fettle and occupying valuable bed space.

Wherever you may be, you will find yourself in the care of a midwife for at least the first ten days of your baby's life. This usually means that for some of that time a community midwife will come into your home. She'll be wearing a blue frock and a natty little hat, and the odds are that she will be a very nice person indeed. She has to be. In and out of people's houses all day long.

Officially she'll come to keep an eye on you and your baby. To make sure that the mildewed luggage label falls neatly off her tummy to leave a thing called a navel. To make sure that your cat isn't sleeping on her face, and to make sure that you are not quietly coming apart at the seams. But if she's anything like the midwives I've known, she'll do a lot of other things as well. Like brewing tea, telling the story of Chicken Licken to your two year old *again*, and talking your dog out of running away to sea.

On her way out on that tenth day, the midwife will leave the door ajar and something called a Health Visitor will slip in. She won't have a uniform so you may mistake her for a Jehovah's Witness. Check this out before you start yelling. After all, Jehovah's Witnesses will usually go quietly if you ask them to. The Health Visitor is a different kettle of fish.

She is highly trained and socially aware, so your best line of defence could well be a safety chain on the door. *However*, she is the first child-orientated professional with whom you will have an on-going relationship. You could do worse than cut your teeth on her, because ahead of you there lie bigger hurdles. Like teachers.

If you've never met a Health Visitor you may be wondering what sort of person would be attracted to the work. Misguidedly you might suppose, as I did, that they are people who have done time with their own children and want to be paid to pass on what they have learned. Not so. There *are* such people. But not many. There's a very good chance that your H V will be a childless woman. And, if she is, how much respect do you think you're going to have for her opinions after you've weathered six months of parenthood?

If your Health Visitor is middle-aged and has been in the service a good while, this at least should be said in her favour – whatever you throw at her, she will have seen it before and worse. She will be unshockable and unflappable, so two cheers for the older, childless Health Visitor. For the younger, childless HV I can feel no such charity. Who does she think she is? How dare she step into your kitchen with a bloom on her cheeks to tell you that children like bright, primary colours? I would have her drummed out of the service and not let back in until she has bags under her eyes.

Health Visitors exist to advise us and police us in our parenting. Which just goes to show what a cowed generation we are. Some families need HVs. I'm talking about parents who feed tiny babies on bottles of tea. Or tie them into their cots for hours. Or jump on them. Most parents don't need HVs. They only serve to raise your blood pressure and sap your confidence, but they are a fact of modern life, so you had better know about them.

One of HV's concerns will be your domestic arrangements. She will want to satisfy herself that you aren't drawing your water from a well or sharing your living quarters with a herd of cattle. If you are, you should expect trouble.

There will be the matter of room temperature. Any child born in hospital will come home thinking the world is hot and airless. This is one very good reason for making an early escape from hospital. The sooner you correct your child's expectations the better for her health and for your gas account. But your HV may not share your spartan attitudes. She will like to see a thermometer hanging on the nursery wall, and even in the middle of August she will tap it and look at you meaningfully. All I ask you to remember is how old the human race is. It pre-dates central heating. I was reared in a house where bedrooms were only heated for the dying. And my father was born in a house where the front door was never shut. Because it wouldn't. If you think Daisy may be lying in a draught, put a hat on her. People without hair lose a lot of heat through the top of the head.

HV will also show a passing interest in your star rating as a housekeeper. If you don't merit even a crossed knife and fork this will be a time when you will need to hold firm. HVs only call once in a while, and your peace of mind is more important than theirs. I know a woman who is rearing two small children in a caravan in the middle of a lunar landscape while her man is building a house. She's broken the spirit of two HVs already, and is prepared to loose a very muddy Alsatian (I forgot to mention him) on the next contender.

If you're not a person who goes in for a great deal of wiping down, this is no time to start. Hygiene is a funny business. Somehow, the more you make of it, the less it comforts you. The more you pursue germs the more you're prey to the idea that they may be winning.

In the days when I knew lots of tiny children, I observed a curious thing. The parents who were deeply committed to wiping and mopping were the ones whose children were constantly laid low with upset tummies. The ones growing up in farmyard conditions had constitutions of iron. And something else. The moppers and wipers had bottles of cleaning fluid for every stain known to man, and they kept them in handy places. Like under the sink. I'm as sure now as I was then that greater danger lurked under those sinks than was ever to be met by rolling on my floor. One bottle will do. Use it sparingly, keep it on a very high shelf, and never mind about impressing HV. She, too, has her flaws. Who's to say what lies festering round the back of her Bendix?

HV will also want to be sure that you are sound in mind and body. She will encourage you to take an active interest in your child's development, and may ask you on her first visit whether you've heard about Bonding.

Bonding is something that had been going on for several million years until a doctor, probably a Frenchman, invented it in the Seventies. It is the peculiar process by which an infant's parents look into her eyes, see her soul, and fall in love with her. It helps ensure that while she's growing up there are people around who care about her. It always used to be optional, like sex, and most children somehow ended up with at least one adult that cared. But nowadays Bonding is obligatory.

You will be invited to make a start when your child is two minutes old, even though what you would really like to do is go to sleep, or eat your way through a Pizza House menu. Your baby will be put into your arms and everyone will stand around waiting for you to bond. This is rather like trying to make love on Horse Guards' Parade during the Trooping of the Colour. If things don't work out, you shouldn't worry. Falling in love takes time. For several days you may not even be able to take in that this child has come to live with you and that she looks like ET. There's no hurry. Eventually things will emerge that will bond you to her. Like the way she looks when she's asleep. Or the way he bums a fiver off you to buy you flowers for Mother's Day.

By the time HV comes on the scene she will expect to see the signs of strong mother–child bonding, and, since the late Seventies, father–child bonding. Fathers are another recent discovery. No doubt at some future date we shall be told of the terrible side effects of fathers, but HV, a woman of the times, will be in favour of them. Especially if they are bonding well. What she won't want to see is any sign of mother–father bonding.

In case you were wondering, you *can* conceive another baby within a month of giving birth. You're not supposed even to be Doing It until they've had you up on the ramps for your six-week service and checked that Everything Is As It Should Be. I suggest, with respect, that, if everything is not as it should be, you will not enjoy doing it and that you should not do what you don't enjoy. But, if you *are* enjoying doing it and you truly want two children under the age of two, then that is your business. I think you're mad, but I am the last person to cast stones.

HV will suggest that your body needs time to recover from each pregnancy, and that you need time to enjoy the child you already have. There's a kernel of good sense in what she says. But, for most women, pregnancy is not an illness. Nor are most parents so dimwitted as deliberately to conceive another child before they are ready. And, no, breastfeeding is not a reliable method of contraception.

But to get back to HV who is sitting on the edge of her chair full of helpful hints. Her greatest concern will be your baby, and how she's getting along.

She'll want to check that she's growing. As the weeks go by Daisy should get heavier, probably in fits and starts. If her weight gain is slow, your Health Visitor may query your feeding methods. She may want to know exactly how much the baby's getting and she may want to call and weigh her regularly. It's not that she wants you to produce a light heavyweight. More a case of satisfying herself that the child isn't ill. Such a pity, though, that she'll always arrive to do the weighing just as you've conned Daisy into taking a nap.

The day will eventually come when you will be considered fit to be let out. It will be when you can steer a pram. If you already have a full licence for the standard supermarket trolley with four left wheels, you will find there's nothing to it. Then, HV will invite you to attend the Baby Clinic. If you live three miles up a dirt track, or have encouraged your mynah bird to call her names, HV may stop calling at your home altogether and be relieved at the thought of seeing you on her own territory in future. But be warned. If you skip clinic she'll be back. With reinforcements.

Baby Clinics are not good news. In fact they are pretty well hell on earth. For a start there is a lot of noise. And a lot of jiggling. Jiggling is what nervous adults do when they're holding a child who is about to start up. There's jiggling over the shoulder, which always leaves an icky patch on your jersey, and there's jiggling on the knee, hallmark of the anxious beginner and prone to damage the Achilles tendon. Real pros jiggle over the arm. To do this properly you walk up and down a lot and pretend to hurl the baby through the clinic window. You *must* only pretend.

This technique is very effective in the short term. It can buy you a bit of time. But eventually the noise will break out, and, when it does, there won't be a lot you can do to stop it. Taking a few clothes off may help. If that doesn't work, try taking off some of the baby's clothes. Babies in clinics are always overdressed.

If, when you've removed her teddy fur snowsuit, her stretch terry pull-ups and her thermal earmuffs, she still looks like a boiled goblin and she still won't shut up, the only thing to do is leave. Leaving means piling all those clothes back on, trouncing her into staying put in her pram and promising to come back another day, and all in front of an audience of cheesy, jiggling women.

At baby clinics you'll meet a lot of very tired women who smell of cheese. This may cheer you up. You may make new friends. The first time I ventured inside a clinic, a large, bald baby threw up all over my feet. She's taller than I am now and her mother is still my best friend. So if you are desperate for social contact, loitering in clinics can be profitable. Sort out a likely-looking friend and ask her if she'd like to call round for a sherry and a Valium.

Otherwise, the best plan with clinics is to get there very early, so that you can be first in and first away. Fit blades to your pram wheels and jockey for pole position on the grid. Desperate times call for desperate measures.

Clinics do things like vaccinations, developmental tests, and filling up wet afternoons.

Vaccinations come mostly in the first year and a half. First for polio, diphtheria, tetanus and whooping cough, and then later for measles. As a parent, I know the agonising that can go on over the whooping cough vaccine. I also know that whooping cough is a terrible thing because I've seen it. And so are all the other diseases that children should be protected from but aren't if their parents play truant from the entire vaccination programme.

Developmental tests aren't nearly so harrowing. They will provide you with some of the best entertainment of your life. Better than anything now showing on Shaftesbury Avenue or Broadway. The idea is to check your child's manipulative and conceptual skills against a projected norm.

Apart from the obvious things like sitting up unaided, walking and aiming straight with a spoon (HV may want to check that your baby can do all these things as well), she will examine closely your baby's physical and intellectual progress. She'll get out a box of bricks, and, while she's checking her manual for what children are supposed to be able to do at eighteen months, Daisy will have built a passable model of Wembly Stadium and be trying to eat the box. Never mind. Let HV play. It's what she's paid for.

If there is anything wrong with your child's development, you will probably be the first to notice. It's one of those funny things about parents. It's called instinct, and, despite all the things that can confuse it, like being too anxious or reading too many silly books, I remain firmly in favour of it.

The highlight of the developmental testing calendar is the hearing test. This involves HV and a Hearing Test Lady, hereinafter referred to as HTL, and they may come to your home to do their stuff. There's no need to go to a lot of trouble. Just raise the portcullis a little and chain up your dangerous animals. They will need the undivided attention of you and your child. Bear this in mind if you have other children around and, as I said, chain them up.

The test begins. Daisy sits on your lap with her back to you. HV sits directly in front of her and engages her with some nasty-looking rattles and a pre-war fluffy bunny. Meanwhile HTL sneaks around the room testing Daisy's hearing by making surprising little noises and seeing whether she notices. If Daisy seems chiefly interested in escaping from the horrid bunny, don't worry about her hearing. Just be thankful that she is already such a sound judge of character.

One day your child will get ill. Usually it will be the night before you're going away from her for the very first time. You'll take it personally. And so you should. What she has picked up is not a bug, but your vibrations of dithering self-doubt. Once you've both crossed this bridge, she can settle down to getting proper illnesses.

This brings me to doctors. Many people feel that the best sort of doctor to have for a child is a doctor who has young children herself. I'm not so sure. Hardly any of them are Miriam Stoppard. Most of them are as neurotic and clueless as the rest of us. If she really does have young children, her judgement will be impaired by lack of sleep, and, if she doesn't, she'll be worried about catching whatever it is that your child has got. My preference is for the kindly, vague, older doctor. He will die rather than interfere and is full of jolly sayings, like 'Up and about in no time!' and 'That's the spirit! Mother knows best!' He knows all too well that most of the things that ail children respond nicely to the Hands Off treatment.

A sick child is usually spotty, pukey or just plain unbearable.

Spots first. All new babies get spotty faces. It's their way of protesting about the parlous state the world is in. Dress her in something clean and try to love her anyway.

New babies also get sore bottoms. A sore bottom, as you may already have discovered, is a cardinal sign of chronic neglect and slipshod parenting, so I hope you're thoroughly ashamed of yourself. The best cure is fresh air. No nappy, all morning, out in the

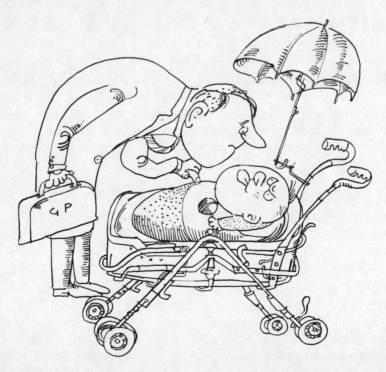

garden. While she's out there taking the air, you can be tracking down the cause. Maybe you're using too much washing powder? Or maybe it's that lotion you've been plastering her with, to stop her getting sore? When you've worked it out you can join her in the garden and see what the fresh air does for you.

Then there are protest rashes. These are usually caused by too many clothes, or silly things like christening gowns. If someone buttoned you into three layers of nylon lace and kept you waiting hours for your tea, wouldn't you do something desperate? O K, so it's a family heirloom. In that case you can comfort yourself that your child's rash has an impeccable pedigree.

Next, the specific spotties.

German Measles is brief, pink and flu-ey. It is impossible to diagnose just by looking, so don't even try.

Chicken Pox is easy. The spots look like little blisters and they itch. Boy, do they itch! You will chiefly want to know when it stops being infectious. Some folks say it's when the last scab has fallen. I'm sorry about this but the word *scab* is something you may as well get used to. Some folks say it's when a one-legged albino osprey crosses your path. Personally, I always found it to be when I was so desperate for the company of other tired, cheesy women that I no longer gave a toss whether their children caught it or not.

Measles is red spots that spread and join up. It's also a heavy cold, a hacking cough and generally feeling beastly. Some children get this one even after being vaccinated. Your doctor may be interested. He may not.

Throwing-up diseases are very common in children, especially if they come from very clean homes. The complaint is usually very short-lived, unless you have insisted on a fortnight in Tunisia, in which case proceed directly to Chapter Twelve, and serve you bloody well right.

A child who is sick or who has the runs wants nothing except to lie very still close to a bucket. She'll get upset about making a mess on her Tigger and Pooh pyjamas and, if she's upset, you must not be. You must not cry because it won't sponge out of the carpet, or because poking the undigested bits down the plughole makes you feel queasy. You are the grown-up now and you must behave like one. Just smile and leave her alone. No food. No nourishing drinks of milk. And no solidifying medicines. Ordinary tummy upsets are self-correcting, and the only help you might think of giving is in replacing some of the lost body fluids. Water or lemonade will do.

Like adults, children suffer from a rag-bag of symptoms that are blamed on viruses. They, too, are usually self-limiting, and the best thing to do is ride them out and leave your doctor time to care for the people who really need him. One of the things a virus infection may do is raise the temperature, and some parents get very anxious when their child gets hot. Don't rush out to buy a thermometer. Where do you think you're going to use it on an uncooperative two year old? There's a marvellous thing you can lay across your child's forehead that will tell you immediately whether he's too hot or not. There's no risk of broken glass, mercury poisoning, or misreading the thing because it was designed by an astigmatic moron. It is called a hand.

And if she is too hot? It means her body is trying to get better. I'd look upon it as a good sign. There are a small number of children who suffer from convulsions when they're feverish. If yours is one of them you may find it comforting to have your doctor call in with his pyjamas showing under his trousers (these things always happen at four in the morning) but there won't be a lot he can do. Except to tell you this. Your child will grow out of it.

The other features of these vague illnesses that do the rounds, is that they leave the sufferer wanting to do nothing at all. If your child gets one of these I do recommend the downstairs bed. Upstairs she'll become a whining pain in the backside, dreaming up things she doesn't really want that you can fetch for her. Downstairs, because she knows you are near, she will be far less demanding. She'll doze on and off, most of the day, and when she's awake she'll have regressed at least a year in intellect. Put away the Flash Cards until she's back on her feet. Better still, put away the Flash Cards for ever. She'll enjoy watching *Play School*, and she'll want lots of cuddles.

Buy her a pack of felt-tip pens and let her while away the hours losing all the tops.

Then there are running repairs. You can do a lot at home with a large reel of sticking plaster. Small children love plasters. They nag endlessly for them and pick them off as soon as they've got them. You *can* tell them that wounds heal faster in the fresh air, which is absolutely true, or you can give in and keep sticking. You can even try drawing faces on the plasters in an attempt to give them a longer life. It all depends on how patient you are, and how often you're prepared to re-stock your medicine cabinet. If you have a medicine cabinet. If I had one I would keep a bottle of witch hazel in it. It's cheap, it has a pretty name, and it's good for bruises and for oily adolescent skins. And if, as in our house, that vital bottle is always empty when you need it, you can raise a whole family of stoics by telling them to buck up and hop bravely.

Anything too big for sticking plaster and a kiss is likely to bring you back into contact with the Professionals again. And there is truly no better place for the sober re-education of parents than a Casualty Department. If you end up in one, you will be full of distracted gratitude towards everyone from the lady with the League of Friends tea trolley to the consultant surgeon with the spotted bow tie. You'll feel a total failure as a parent and go home resolved to make the world a safer place for all children. When you get there, you may need to relieve yourself of your bottled-up anxiety, by knocking seven bells out of your darling child. And, in strict compliance with Sod's Law, this will be the very moment that your Health Visitor decides to drop in and see how you're all getting along.

This is very important. Discipline is a terrible word these days. It smacks of short rations, cold showers and the cat o'nine tails. I am wholly in favour of all of them, because the world is filling up with a breed of disorderly youth such as it has never seen before and, if we are to be saved, we must act at once.

Do not be lulled by the idea that youth has always been insufferable. In olden days its beastliness was kept within certain bounds. Things like rickets and cholera and conditions at t'Mill stopped them well short of total lawlessness. After they had risen at dawn, been soundly beaten in exchange for a bowl of gruel and then queued an hour to use the privy, they had no energy for robbing the old and resisting education. And, for those that weren't at Eton, it was not much better. Life was a patchwork of cold rooms, gristly mutton and senseless adult violence.

Then, around about 1946, there was a change of heart. I shan't dwell on the consequences of Welfare orange juice because that's a long time ago now. That crowd are well past adolescence and coasting downhill to the menopause. But Welfare orange is a symbol. It marks a great social upheaval that transformed the child from a despised public nuisance into a feared and cosseted lapdog. We stopped enduring children and encouraged them to become rampant consumers and arbiters of taste and public decency. In the Eighties, to deny a child anything has become a matter for grave consideration.

If you're new to children the first thing you may notice about them is their size. They are enormous. I blame it on central heating. And oven chips. Boys and girls alike, they are built like armoured pissoirs. Making it difficult for the average parent, desk-bound all day and a life member of Weightwatchers by night, to get the upper hand.

The answer is to start young. If we are to be able to collect our pittance of a pension free of the fear of armed robbery, we have to catch the next lot before they are out of nappies, and reduce them to terrified submission. I hope I may have caught you at the start of parenthood. There is no better time to alarm you. He may be a warm, delightful little armful today, but a year or two on he will be starting to change. And, because you have fallen in love with him, he may dupe you into believing that he personifies bright, unfettered youth, and that it's all the others who are on the road to ruin.

At the beginning, all it takes is a little awareness. A new baby doesn't need disciplining. This is the time when you should be putting your feet up and conserving your strength for the ear-splitting battles that come later. I know what you're thinking. What about all that yelling? If he yells and we run to see, isn't he learning that yelling gets him his own way? Won't he have us dancing on a string forever? The playthings of a cunning, manipulative tyrant? No. Let me remind you how a baby works.

Babies are at everyone's mercy. Put yourself in their bootees, unable to get about or make yourself understood. If you have your health, *you* are able to see to your own needs. If you have a thirst you can totter across to El Vino's and get it catered for. If you are suffering from pressure in the bowel, you can tell the switchboard you're *in conference* for half an hour and disappear with your copy of *The Listener*. Your baby can only cry. Communication is the name of the game and, if you run to see every time he opens his mouth, the system is working well.

Manipulation and tyranny come later. If you listen carefully to instinct while Vlad the Impaler is tiny and vulnerable, the same instinct will alert you to any shift in circumstances, and the first time he makes unreasonable demands, you will feel it in your gut.

As soon as this happens, you must put Discipline on standby and face something difficult. You are dealing with a very small child. Because of this you should keep discipline on a simple footing. At this stage, it helps to have rules that are clear-cut and severe. There is no point in diluting it or discussing it with a two year old, because you've been round longer than he has, you're bigger than he is, and anyway he's not articulate enough for an argument.

Your first fight will usually be over some measly material possession that he wants to destroy and you want to preserve. Stereo systems are a great favourite. So are video recorders. They are magnetic to the newly mobile human.

Some people put everything away in cardboard boxes as soon as they know they are pregnant, and reckon on leaving it all in the loft until after Vlad has left home. They decide it's not fair to expect a child to understand. I cannot agree. Children cannot expect adults to go for years on end without gadgets and knobs and switches. How about a little understanding for the bigger folks? Day after day we pack ourselves into trains full of communicable diseases. We face up to armpit odour, the falling pound, and the grim reality of earning a crust. Are we to be denied the pleasure of playing with our toys? Must we really live without electrical twiddly bits because Vlad the Lad can't leave them alone? Of course not. All you need are a few rules about knobs. You should take him to one side and tell him in a confident tone that he must not touch. And, while you've got him there, tell him what will happen if he does.

When our children were very young, we couldn't afford a stereo. We took turns with an inverted tumbler against next door's wall and were just thankful to have a mangle that was in good working order. Later on, we scraped a few quid together and signed up for the fleshpots. That was when the children had to learn. If they even breathed on those knobs, they got The Works. A real Oscar-winning performance. And it did work. The only trouble we have ever had with twiddlers has been with other people's children, and with adults who said we were not properly tuned. But that is another story.

There are many methods of bringing children to heel. Some, like physical force and hot pursuit, involve a loss of dignity by all concerned. I would keep those as a last resort. Try something less strenuous first.

You *can* discipline a child using only your voice and your eyes. If you practise often enough, the child will eventually be so sensitive to your opinions that you can forget about the voice and rely on the eyes alone. You will need to prepare yourself for this.

Sit in front of your mirror and look yourself in the eye. Say to yourself, 'I weigh one hundred and forty pounds, I make thirteen thousand a year, and I *can* do this.' Don't be shifty about it and don't look away when you say the word *can*. Next, give your voice an airing. How does it sound? Does it sound like it means business? Does it register on the Richter Scale? Cowardice constricts the throat, and so does wavering intent. That voice is going to have to come from your feet. It must start as a rumble in the ground you are fighting to hold, and it must be helped on its way through an expanded chest and a relaxed throat. You will find it helps to have Strepsils and an unshakeable faith in your own moral rectitude. Used this way the human voice can stop a child dead in its tracks.

I don't want to hear about your grumbling appendix or your nervous disposition. You can't possibly be any weedier than I was when I started, and, if you suffer with your nerves, you should never have had children. Keep practising.

Roaring is all very well in the privacy of your own double-glazed moorland retreat, but on your way round Safeway's on a Saturday morning you may be glad of something more subtle. None of us likes to lose face in public, and taking on a wayward child is one of those situations, like lying in a pool of blood, that draws a crowd in seconds. You'll attract the same bunch of ghouls if you try to give birth or complain about shoddy goods. On many occasions I've seen a parent start well and then back off when the glare of the spotlight got too much. In these days of the Children's Charter no one will ever back you up, or offer to hold him for you while you take aim. Apart from me, and I can't be everywhere at once.

What you need is something unobtrusive. A silent but effective way of telling him that if he doesn't do exactly as he's told he will rue it for the rest of the week. This is where the eyes come in. You

must learn to speak with them. It's not terribly British, but there we are. Back to the mirror.

Put your face right up to it, narrow your eyes and think *power*. Breathe deeply and let it come through. Think of the most thwarted moments in your life. Re-live your worst humiliations at the hands of women in nail varnish. Now re-write them. Cast yourself as the victor and let the triumph show in your eyes. Children are very susceptible to this. If you try it on an adult who's used to seeing you dither, he'll probably ask you what you've been taking, and is there any chance of you getting some for him? But a child will just jump.

You can use the eyes on their own, or combined with the quiet, purposeful voice and the firmly held wrist. It's entirely up to you. But you have to believe in what you're doing. I've had marvellous results with children who were total strangers. It might have been

the garlic on my breath. But I think it was the sheer shock of being spoken to urgently by an adult with crazy eyes. I don't think the mechanics of it matter. Just as long as Vlad is left in no doubt that, if he carries on like that a minute longer, he will be struck by a thunderbolt.

How are you placed for thunderbolts? Me neither. They seem to have gone the way of Gregory Powders and blancmange. I must now make it clear that I do not advocate a return to the cane and the tawse. Those who do, have their reasons. Provided they don't turn up at one of my fork suppers with a bag full of accoutrements, I'll say no more. But I do think the rolled up *Radio Times* has fallen into sad disuse. It was discreet, easy to store, cheap to replace and without equal for so many distasteful household tasks. Handy for puppy-bonking, wasp-swatting and child-swiping *and* for telling you the time of *Yesterday in Parliament*. A parent's *vade mecum* if ever there was one. Used on the thigh of a four year old who won't shape up, it will cause temporary redness and a tactical withdrawal. I always aimed below the waist. If necessary I consolidated my position by then lifting the child by his lapels until his feet were well clear of the ground. If he had no lapels, in the name of symmetry I used the *Radio Times* on his other leg.

You must never be afraid to get physical with your children. A fight to the death on the sitting-room floor can save a thousand words. Go for something that suits your style. I can never manage rugby tackles, but I'm good at pinning them flat on their backs until I get a submission. And you haven't seen anything until you've seen me do the mother of four who has been pushed too far and has gone into uncontrolled orbit.

What I like about slogging it out on the shag pile is that it clears the air quickly. Anything less immediate needs thinking through very thoroughly. If fear of losing face is fatal to discipline in public, inability to follow through will wreck it at home. If you send him to bed early, are you really going to keep him there till morning? If you say no TV, are you going to send him out of the room while you see how you fared in the 3.30 at Newmarket? Does No Sweets include the ones Granny has brought him all the way from Kidderminster? And does not speaking to him for an hour hold out even when he has hold of your leg and tells you that fat ladies are what he likes best? Worst of all, are you guilty of making an Idle Threat?

Here is an Idle Threat.

Idle Threatener: Stop that and come here at once.
Vlad: Vroooooom . . .
IT: If you don't stop that and come here at once there will be trouble.
Vlad: Mmmmmmmmmmm. Pow! Splat! Vroooom . . .
IT: I'm going to count to five.
Vlad: Nnnnneeeeeeeeow. Aaaaaaargh! Brmmmmmmmmm.
IT: One . . . Two . . . Three . . . Four . . . Four and a half . . .

Four and three quarters . . .
*Time then stands still. Vlad carries on until he has re-enacted all
the scenes from Flash Gordon that have occurred to him and he
feels the need to sit down quietly.*
IT: That's better. Now be a good boy and we'll see what the ice-
cream van might have.

Children can smell the impotence of an Idle Threat a mile off.
They know that the count will never reach five, and the man with
the big stick will never show up. One child rumbled it years ago and
the word just got around.

We have someone in our house who makes Idle Threats. I'm not
prepared to say who it is. All I will say is that, when he claims he's
going to lock the person who writes on walls, in their bedroom *for a
hundred years*, the other one of us reaches for the rolled-up *Radio
Times* and deals summarily with anyone she catches sniggering.

It's no good. You must say what you are going to do and then do
it.

Family disputes *can* be dealt with the same way as disputes
anywhere else. You can all sit down at a family council and thrash it
out. Everyone can have a turn at putting their point of view,
everyone else can tell them how wrong they are, and then the
meeting can be adjourned until someone puts a better offer on the
table. Family councils are an excellent introduction to democracy in
the rough. The frustrations and the time and energy consumed by
all that futile repetition show up the cracks better than O-level
British Constitution ever could. Family councils confirmed for me
something I first suspected years ago – that we are all closet tyrants
at heart.

The easiest disputes to resolve are the ones between children. The
balance of power between brothers and sisters is a volatile thing. You
never know quite where it is or how it may flare up. Size and age have
no bearing upon it, and you will find that each of your children is as
capable as the other of foul, unscrupulous behaviour. The quickest
solution is to unite them against a common enemy. You.

Just make an unfair, high-handed announcement that affects them both, and leave them to do the rest themselves. It works like a dream. As they search Yellow Pages for the number of the nearest Old People's Home, and weigh up their chances of succeeding with a mutiny, their differences will be forgotten. The larger the family, the better this works. And it is wonderfully satisfying to see such solidarity. It encourages you to hope that when you have retired to a Twilight Home on the Côte d'Azur, they will still look out for one another.

But, of course, the majority of quarrels are not between children. Mostly they are temporary discrepancies between the way the child wants to behave and the way some stingy adult says things have to be. Some of them are perennial. Like never putting anything away. Some are spur of the moment. Like swearing.

Some parents treat everything the same way. They scream and throw Capo di Monte. Or they say in a very tired voice, 'We'll see what your mother has to say about this when she gets home.'

I think it helps to separate your complaints into categories. Hitting a six into next door's greenhouse isn't going to happen every day. Leaving roller skates on the stairs and not flushing the lavatory are. These are chronic problems, and the answer to them is re-education. Throwing a tantrum may relieve the pressure behind your eyeballs, but it will not prevent the episode being repeated. To do that you have to re-programme them.

I have a confession to make. I know a lot about the theory of re-education, but I have had very little practical experience. I am often too tolerant and regularly too tired to carry the scheme through to completion. I just erupt into window-rattling fury once a month, and they all go quiet and allude to my hormones. But I have seen abler parents than I nip bad habits in the bud. Here is what they do. They make a pre-emptive strike.

Instead of waiting for the sin to be committed, they pounce while the child is still thinking about something else. If they wish to put a stop to coats being dropped one yard inside the front door, they lie in wait for the culprit and apprehend him before he's even started to unbutton. Then they take him through the desired behaviour pattern, step by step. They walk him straight past his happy dumping ground and on, until he stands before the coat peg. Until he gets there he's not allowed to so much as touch a button. Then, when he has hung up his coat and his scarf and his rugby boots, they reward him with a welcoming smile and the offer of a cup of tea. The next day they go through the whole business again. That way he learns to hang up his coat the same way that he learned to cross the road and hold a knife and fork. By doing it day after day, the right way. It's time consuming, but it does work and it's easier on the Capo di Monte.

Sporadic problems like swearing, and breaking things, and threatening to leave home can only be dealt with as they arise. You can't plan ahead. If you could, you could say now that when one of your children breaks something your response will depend on whether you can call it fair wear and tear, or a complex plot to dismantle the whole house around your ears. But you'll find instead that it's the chipped cup that pushes you over the edge.

I *know* that everyone has accidents. I *know* that possessions are a degrading obsession for a woman blessed with good health. But I still find myself sitting on the kitchen floor shouting, 'How come none of you has ever wanted for *Star Wars* stickers and I've been waiting for a new milk jug since 1981?'

If the damage is minor and genuinely could not be helped, you will do yourself a big favour by setting to quietly with a dustpan and brush and being jolly decent about the whole affair. It will strengthen your case enormously when something else makes you crack and you dock all pocket money until the damage is repaired.

Leaving home is a more delicate problem. My biggest worry is that no one ever tries to stop me. When the children threaten to do it, we always let them go through with the packing. It's so interesting to see what treasures they feel they cannot live without. And to see how similar they are to the things I planned to lug all the way to Llangollen back in 1959 (everything ever written by Angela Brazil, a lump of Mount Etna, my Post Office book and, with heavy heart, a photograph of all the people who used to love and understand me).

When they've packed, we have them in for a quick word about travel arrangements, and to tell them that we'd be really pleased if they'd reconsider – even though, less than an hour before, one of us has told them to go and never darken our door again.

Which brings me back to adults. And inconsistency. Before we had children I liked books that told you what was what. Books that said children need rules. Clear, reasonable rules, to be followed by everyone, at all times. No evasions. No exceptions.

I'm not so keen on rules any more. Except for the very young and the very cowed I have found rules to be a nuisance. They got recited back to me at awkward moments. They cornered me. And there I was trying to deal with things on an *ad hoc* basis. We dumped most of the rules.

This left us room for the arbitrary decision, irrationality and unfairness. And it struck us what a marvellous foretaste of life we were giving our children. If you don't tell Vlad about half-truths, rule-benders and outright villainy before his eighteenth birthday, the world is going to come as a terrible shock to him. If you've lumbered yourself with a book full of rules, it can get very difficult when you need to arrange a bit of laissez-faire without looking a perfect fool. We parents need room to manoeuvre.

Swearing is a fine example of what I mean. Along with working a sixty-hour week, repaying a crippling mortgage and generally abusing my body, swearing is something I choose to do. I consider it a privilege of adult life. But I prefer my children not to do it. They don't understand the words, and I don't like the way it reflects on me, if they go around using them. On this point and others I am an unapologetic hypocrite.

Another thing about rules is that the rule-makers have to be of one mind, or at least be prepared to say that they are. If you are the sort of couple who always agree on principle, this is easy. You must just hope that your children will have twice as much respect for two adults who are wrong as they would have had for one. And, if you are both unsure of yourselves, sticking together is undoubtedly the best policy. In the dark, it is always best to cling to something friendly. But, if she thinks *she* has the answer, and you know for certain *you* have the answer, I think it is best to say so. Children see straight through gritted teeth and ominous looks. Far better to say, 'We have a rule that no one eats pasta away from the table but, on the occasion of *Ski Sunday* being broadcast at an inconvenient time, your father is prepared to waive the death penalty for meat sauce on the Dralon. And on his own Flokati rug be it!'

This sort of situation will demonstrate to your children all they will ever need to know about discipline. That rules always show up when you least need them. That there are always two ways of looking at everything, including Thou Shalt Not Kill. And that all you, as a parent, are trying to do, in your fumbling uncertainty, is turn them into the kind of people you wouldn't mind being trapped in a lift with.

If you are new parents there's no need to join the catering corps right away. Until your child is about six months old, she'll only want milk. This will give you time to decide whether your destiny is in the ranks, or whether you are genuine officer material.

First let me tell you about milk. It comes in breasts or bottles, and provided you have breasts, the choice is yours. If you are flat-chested and wear Y-fronts you are, by an accident of birth, restricted to bottles. If you're just flat-chested, I can assure you that, when the moment comes, the equipment will appear, so buy yourself a 40C cup and wait for a novel experience.

Whichever method of getting milk into your baby you decide upon, you'll have questions you want to ask, and here is the first golden rule. Never ask an expert. And never read a book by an expert, unless they tell you on the first page that they have actually done the thing themselves.

I can't tell you anything about bottle-feeding because I was too idle ever to try it, but there are thousands of people who have. Choose someone you like, who has happily bottle-fed at least one baby, and address all your questions to them.

I *can* tell you about breast-feeding. And so can lots of other people who have done it. It's very simple. After your baby is born, your breasts make milk, and babies like the taste of it. What is even more amazing, the more milk your baby drinks, the more your body makes. It is sheer magic. The other thing you should know is that breast milk looks nothing like the stuff you get off a United Dairies float. Breast milk looks weak and watery by comparison and certain people may look over your shoulder and remark on this. Ignore their gross impertinence and carry on regardless – unless you are wet-nursing a Hereford calf – in which case you should panic. And, if you must read a book about it, read someone like Sheila Kitzinger. Her *Experience of Breast Feeding* is guaranteed to make the biggest duffer on earth feel beautiful, clever and confident.

I've said this before but I'll say it again, because you didn't believe me the first time. Until she's six months old, all she needs is milk. Truly. She can get along nicely without steak and kidney pudding. Throughout those six months well-meaning people will keep suggesting that it's time for her to have a little extra something or other, but you should tell them to go away – even though you are as eager as they are to move on to the next stage of feeding – because boredom with milk is no good reason. Parents do a lot of things out of boredom. 'He needs a babywalker,' they say. What they mean is, it's a wet Saturday afternoon and they feel like using their Barclaycard. If you're bored, try changing the colour of your eyeshadow, but leave the baby to her milk.

But what about vitamins, I hear you ask? What about beri-beri? And impaired fertility in the rat? Don't fret. Your Health Visitor will provide you with vitamin drops, and then it's up to you to drop them into something, like a bottle of boiled water or a spoon. Somehow ours always managed to drop out of reach behind the fridge and gather fluff, and somehow our children stayed robust and healthy.

You might be tempted by one of those vitamin-enriched syrups for diluting and feeding to your baby as a drink. Don't, unless the label is quite categoric about it containing no sugar. Most of them do contain sugar, and, though they may taste really yummy and enable you to buy useful things by saving up the labels and sending a stamped, addressed envelope, your baby will find them addictive, and her teeth, which have yet to see the light of day, will be ruined by them. She will drink water. Boiled water at first, and then just plain old tap water. But, if she once acquires the taste for sugar, you are sunk.

As the six-month marker looms, you may start to think about what to feed the beast. If you have so far lived happily on carry-outs and Mars Bars, this may be your first encounter with a thing called a sieve. If you're in a higher income bracket, the thing will be called a food processor, but don't let this go to your head. The chief difference between the two is speed. A food processor works twenty times faster and takes a thousand times longer to clean.

Sieving can be a real drag. At the beginning it's fun pushing Lamb Rogan Josh through all those little holes, but one cupful lasts forever and you can end up with a fridge full of fur-coated cups. I'm told the thing to do is put little dollops of the stuff into ice-cube trays in the freezer. Then, when they're frozen, flip them out, bag them up and label them. That way you end up with a store of frozen meal-sized portions, and your cups stay in circulation.

If you want your child to eat what you eat right from the start, you have to keep it all as free of salt and sugar as you can and bash the lumps out of it. But if, after due consideration, you reckon that Rita can wait a while before she tastes your Goulash with Sour Cream, you can say, 'Sod the sieve,' and move on to jars.

There are jars and there are jars. Some have very appealing titles, and some have things in them that don't taste too good – a fact which, according to the manufacturers, should not discourage us from feeding them to people too young to write letters of complaint. The thing that all jars have in common is this. You take them off the shelf, ease the lid off, and dinner is served. And, as a woman who has sieved her way through the inedible and the impossible, I must say this. I like jars.

Breasts and jars can make travelling with a small baby a fairly simple matter. You just strap her to the back of your tandem and go. When she gets hungry you stop and feed her and then, as soon as the little indicator on her eyeballs is back to the mark that says Full, you can snap the lid back on the jar, re-arrange your vest, and press on with your journey. No need for primus stoves, in-car rotisserie spits, or the common charity of the man in the street. And just as well. The British are the most inept race on earth when it comes to catering for the very young. Italians moisten their lips with Barolo and sing to them. Americans build whole chains of eating houses just to please them. And even the French, who have a proud history of being mean to children, have them wheedling escargots out of their shells before they are out of nappies. But try to feed a British baby in public and someone will fetch a policeman.

So jars and the occasional bit of private enterprise that doesn't call for a sieve – I'm thinking here of those evergreen standbys for us squaddies of the catering corps, the mashed banana and the soft-boiled egg yolk – will get you by for a couple of months. Make the most of the mashed banana phase. It will be the only time in your life you can get rid of bananas that have gone black and squishy. Ever afterwards these are the ones that will, like the bruised apples and the oranges that don't come fitted with zip fasteners, be studiously avoided by the whole family.

The next thing you know, Rita will get teeth. And when a lass has got teeth she wants to use them. She wants lumps. If your cooking is anything like mine, this will be when you really come into your own. Lumps are dead easy. You can make them without even meaning to. The only decisions to be made are what size they're to be and what they're to taste of.

People say children learn to eat and accept whatever they are offered. They swear that their children like nothing better than Chicken Liver Mousse and Sprouted Alfafa. I can't understand this. My children have eaten their way through every cookery book known to man. Together we have been adventurous in delicatessens and gazed hopefully into hypermarket freezers. And do you know what they like best? How right you are. They like them with sausages, they like them with eggs. They like them with nothing more than salt and vinegar, and, given the chance, they'd like them with rhubarb crumble. They *will* eat other things if pushed, but anything with bones in it, or anything green is prodded suspiciously unless, and here is an important point, unless it has been cooked by a thing called A Granny.

If you have a granny in the family, ask it to whip up a quick dish of sheep's eyeballs in strychnine sauce, and watch your child lick the pattern off her plate. And if her glasses aren't too steamed up, watch for the glint in Granny's eye. There's another thing about grannies and food. A granny will coax a reluctant eater. She'll get her to clear her dish and find Peter Rabbit under the gravy. It does save a lot of waste, but as a tactic I disapprove of it. I don't think children should know the power of having an adult cutting up mouthfuls of food and cajoling them to eat one more spoonful for Teddy. It gives them a look that says 'See! How neglected I've been!' and it brings that terrible glint back to Granny's eyes.

This is a good time to talk about how much trouble you should go to for children. We live in child-orientated times. It is no longer done to view childhood as an imperfect and anti-social phase best

got through as quickly as possible. I'm not advocating sending them back down the mines. Just asking them to carry in the odd bucket of coal. And not sheltering them from every inconvenience. Maybe you won't agree. Maybe you're the sort of parent that is prepared to make frogman-shaped fishcakes to try to tempt Rita into eating a mite of haddock? But if she has you hovering solicitously while she toys with her frogman fishcake, what's she going to be like in twenty years time? Are you turning her into the sort of woman who can only look at grapes if all the pips have been removed? Will she ever be fit to live with?

Actually, tiddling up food hardly ever works. I never met a child who would eat tiddled fish if she wouldn't eat it straight. Piped rosettes and sprinkled hundreds and thousands will not distract her from the fact that she has met a taste she doesn't like, and if she won't eat her fricassée because it's a dead chicken laid out under a blanket of milk and flour, the situation will not be retrieved by tomato waterlilies.

Attitudes to food run very deep. It isn't just a matter of how hungry we are and what's in the cupboard. The more trouble the cook has gone to, the more applause and appreciation he needs, and for many women there is an unspoken link between making a good job of nourishing others and being a good person.

Consider the imagery of home baking. The very words conjure up a type of woman, and a comforting smell. One of the first complaints my children made when I took up paid work outside the home was that they never had warm cake for tea any more. Their cries failed to move me. The truth of the matter was that my cakes had always been so appalling that the children had hidden pieces of them under their beds rather than eat them. The house was crawling with mouldering Dundee. What they were missing was the idea of a woman with flour on her hands and the kettle on the hob.

We all fall for silly ideas sometimes. Like making our own bread because that's a really homey thing to do – even though dough scares the hell out of us and we just know it's never going to rise. Or going all out for a truly traditional Christmas. Spending October and November making bread sauce, cranberry sauce, and anything else you can foist onto a turkey who's past caring, and finding, come Christmas Day, that you'd all rather have a cheese sandwich and watch *Morons from Outer Space*.

Have a think about what you do in the kitchen. Work out who you're doing it for and whether it's worth it. I stopped tiddling a long time ago, the day we dumped the rosette nozzles and the frogman templates. I thoroughly recommend it.

Once she can sit up, your child can learn what a table is for. You can start with a high chair. A high chair is a well-designed crud collector. The more elaborate it is, the more scope there will be for things to land in the crevices and set very hard. You can get high chairs that convert to low chairs, high chairs that convert to baby walkers that convert to garden swings, and all of them will, without effort on your part, convert to insanitary harbourers of gunge. The best thing is to get a secondhand one and move on as swiftly as possible to an ordinary chair and a washable cushion. She'll fall off it from time to time, but what's new? Grown men regularly fall off their chairs at my table. If they're still hungry we pick them up. If they've had enough, and they usually have, we leave them where they are.

The other thing is to leave the Spode and the Waterford crystal until later. Don't postpone it indefinitely because, if she ever gets invited to the Guildhall, she'll need to know that plates don't bounce, but just for a start give her equipment that she can throw overboard without doing any damage.

If she sits with you at mealtimes, she'll soon get the idea that a table is a place where there's space for food and drink, but not for feet and not for At-At or the Flower Fairies.

I like tables. I like to sit at them, eat good things and talk to good people. I insist that my children allow this. When they understand these terms, they are welcome to join me. And they nearly always do. Other people's children are another matter. Mostly they give me indigestion. I blame all this on psychologists and finger painting. Many parents fear that they will permanently scar their child's psyche by making him sit still on his chair. Understandably, Kevin therefore feels that he may go walkabout with his meatballs. Furthermore, he will want to share the texture of each dish with the person nearest to him, because in pre-school playgroups, feeling the texture is the name of the game. I avoid other people's children at table as much as I can. The only place I've not had a lot of luck with this policy is at birthday parties.

These cannot be avoided for ever. You may do things like arranging for all your children to have birthdays during the two weeks in August when everyone goes to Bournemouth, but sooner or later you'll have to have a party, and food will be involved.

Most party food does not get eaten. Most of it ends up underfoot. First, guess how much food you'll need, divide it by ten, take away the number you first thought of, and you'll still have too much. Second, get Berger to colour-match it with your carpet. Third, did you have parties when you were a kid and did your Mum make bunny rabbit jellies and sandwiches with smiley faces? So did mine. Forget it. Fourth, don't get too clever.

Our most disastrous party was a Hallowe'en-cum-Guy Fawkes do. Our in-house children dressed up in so much green face paint and stick-on running sores that many of their friends were too scared to come in. Then the food backfired. We made black ice-cubes with frozen Coca-Cola and everyone said could they have a glass of plain milk, if it wasn't too much trouble; and the ice-cream and chocolate-flake bonfire cake went down like a lead balloon, and because it was melting we couldn't even get rid of it by sending it home wrapped in Scooby Doo serviettes.

I should have known better. Birthday cakes are a real waste of time, because no one ever wants to eat them. I used to take this personally until I realised that the cake my children brought home from other people's parties didn't get eaten either. The candles are what they like. Stick the right number of candles in a lump of plasticine and they'll be just as pleased. It's the number of times you're prepared to re-light the candles that counts. Let everyone present have at least one go at blowing them out and you will be voted Partygiver of the Year.

I'd put this piece of sound advice into practice myself only I'm through with parties. I've done my share. Hedgehog Cakes, Alligator Cakes, Clock Cakes. The year I did the Steam Engine Cake the fire brigade helped. Eight burly men, desperate for a cup of tea after putting out my neighbour's fire, sat in my kitchen and made the bogeys out of Rolos and cocktail sticks. Then there was the year we tried for a green helicopter and didn't put it in a high place while the icing set. The dog ate it *and* the silver cake board it stood on, so we had to do a bit of quick thinking the next day. And thinking on your feet isn't easy when you've been up all night seeing to a dog with silver and green diarrhoea.

When you're planning the party food, work on the assumption that each time a child wins a small chocolate bar as a prize, he will eat it. Then empty as many bags of crisps as you can afford into a trough. If you absolutely must cook something, let it be sausages, and serve them cold. Otherwise, stick to crisps. Crisps and fizzy pop. Plenty of fizzy. If you use paper cups, and who wouldn't, a lot of the pop will end up on the Disneyland paper tablecloth, so buy lavishly. And relax. Few of your little guests will stay seated at the table. Mostly they will do fast-approach mid-air refuels with Hula Hoops, and stand still only long enough to wet their knickers or be sick.

But back to proper food. I wouldn't want to give the impression that I'm in favour of bullying at the table, because I'm not. Quite the contrary. I've seen many decent people bullied into ulcers and loss of appetite by small, bumptious children and I think someone should put a stop to it. We should all safeguard our future good digestion by insisting on a few simple favours from those who eat with us. No animal impersonations. No walking on the table. Then you can afford to be accommodating about the details.

If Rita doesn't fancy the lumps you've offered her and says she'll just eat bread, never mind. Whatever she doesn't eat there'll be something else in her diet that will compensate, so disengage your brain from the problem of how to get her to eat carrots, and find something substantial to worry about. Flexibility. That's what you need.

Flexibility is very handy. It lets you make up the rules as you go along, and can strengthen your case when you suddenly want to be bossy and unreasonable. For instance, you can be flexible about mealtimes without damaging your health. When I was a child I hated Sundays. Sundays I never saw my mother. She stayed in the kitchen with a lot of steam and angst. Sundays meant gravy browning and lunch on the table at one. If she didn't maintain standards, who would? Not me. I would like my children to regard food as a simple privilege and pleasure. On Sundays we have Tenses in bed and then High Trunch at four.

Once your child is table-trained, you can show her that eating doesn't have to mean tables and chairs. Grass is great and so are beaches. Ankle-deep in salt water with the August rain dripping off her sou'-wester, Rita will eat *anything*.

Eating in cars is trickier. We still haven't perfected it, after years of trying. Somehow, even dry crackers end up sticky, so you should only do it when there is really no alternative. I can remember an especially tacky Easter Sunday morning dash to Gatwick, when I determinedly served sausages from a thermos *and* we had Easter eggs while everyone changed into clothes suitable for meeting a granny – all in the space of a modest estate car. This was parental folly of the worst kind, and I hope that by admitting to it I may save you from a similar experience. Nowadays we'd arrange a bank loan and go to a Happy Eater.

Finally we should talk about children and kitchens. If you've fitted one of those little Alcatraz gates across the doorway to keep you in and the juniors out, the day will come when he steps over it and says, 'Can I help?' If he's taller than you, show him where you keep the gin and the quails eggs and tell him you'll have it on a tray in the bath. If he's younger you'll have to think of something less ambitious. Let me tell you the sort of thing.

In the beginning you must keep it really simple. There is nothing worse than starting to make something you don't want and you don't need, and then finding that he's lost interest and wandered off to play marbles. Today's child is a push-button child. He wants instant results. And, though I do believe that he should learn that life isn't always like this, I don't think the kitchen is the ideal place to teach it.

If you think he'll want to be eating within five minutes of having thought of doing some cooking, you'll do better to ask him to wait until it's time for you to cook the next meal and then let him have a little hand in that. He can try cracking an egg into a cup. As long as it's not your very last egg on half-day closing. Or he can measure something into a jug. After that he may be quite content to get back to his Fuzzy Felt.

If he's been to a playgroup or a nursery class, it may be a different story. These places encourage children to demand hands-on experience of everything. Even if someone built your kitchen in a small cupboard and you're under the doctor with your nerves, enthusiasts will tell you that he'll learn a lot of worthwhile things about weight and volume and manual dexterity. And I can tell you that he will also learn what *Hot* means. And words like *Bugger*.

Playgroups go in for kitchen play that will give the child a meaningful learning experience right up to the armpits. Things like peppermint creams. They don't require any cooking, but they use up icing sugar by the lorryload, and they are not fit to eat. Nor is the pastry. I should tell you that it will take a whole pile of grey pastry to ensure that your child grows up well-rounded and unrepressed.

When your children are old enough to have learned about heat and knives and snarling adults, they can help out in the kitchen by doing the jobs you hate. Like chopping parsley, or grating carrots. Or making up his packed lunch for the next day. Naturally, he will abuse your trust in him at first, but eventually he'll tire of chocolate-spread sandwiches. Allowing him to do it himself will at least put an end to him complaining that the other lumberjacks snigger at his Marmite soldiers.

After he's done a bit of dogsbodying for you, if he's still keen, he can have a go at things that will pass for meals. Start him on Pot Noodles, Non-Bake Cheesecake, Things on Toast and Things in Pitta Bread. When he's got the hang of those he'll be well on the way to not starving in a bedsit and coming home with a bag of dirty shirts over his emaciated arm every weekend. And you will be on the way to finding yourself back on the right side of the Alcatraz gate eating your fish supper out of newspaper, for old times' sake.

6 *Serviceable Shades of Grey*

Is your airing cupboard full of soft, springy piles of baby clothes in strong, true colours? Is there an outfit for every occasion, and is every morning like Christmas? How lovely. Your child is young. You are in control. During the next twelve years your child will hate, in turn, high-necked jumpers, long socks, short socks, socks, things that are tight round the middle, things that are loose round the middle, and absolutely anything brown. But we should begin at the beginning.

People start to give you baby clothes the day after your pregnancy test is positive. After that it's like Ravel's Bolero. It goes on for a very long while and ends in a frenzy of tissue paper parcels and eau de nil bonnets. You can have worked for five years opposite the most paedophobic grouch under the sun, and suddenly he'll drag out a piece of startlingly pink knitting and insist that it's nothing much. You will be swamped by pastel knits. Perfect strangers will have sweated blood over them. And it's a crying shame, because, even if you try really hard, you'll have difficulty making sure every one of them gets a wearing. Think of them not so much as clothes, more as little woolly messages of welcome. Damn it all, a glut of mittens is not such a bad start in life. The world will be queueing up to tread on his fingers soon enough. Of course, if people ask you what you'd like, you can suggest something more useful, like a new gearbox for the expectant mother's car, or a down payment on the lad's first pair of shoes. And, if they insist that it has to be something knitted, you can always commit it to mothballs. Sooner or later someone else will have a positive pregnancy test, and you'll be glad of a bit of mint condition handknitting to wrap in tissue paper.

Gifts apart, what you should look for in first stage clothing is tough simplicity. New babies leak like sieves. Down their trousers, up their vests, and silently but steadily down their fronts. If yours seems particularly bad, check that you're holding him the right way up.

Because he won't keep anything dry for five minutes at a time, it's important that whatever he wears is easy to put on, easy to take off and indestructible in the washtub. It is hard to improve on those stretchy boiler suits with feet. They're warm, practical and fasten by one of the simplest of modern inventions, the popper. Poppers are such a doddle that when you're on the night shift you can do the whole business and never open your eyes.

In one of these outfits the lad can't fail to look smart. You can pick him up and throw him around, there are no difficulties working out where his hand-embroidered sheet ends and his nightwear begins, and unless he's been wearing it for more than a couple of hours you can be fairly certain that any leakages will be, as they say in the Nuclear Reactor movies, in a containment situation. Personally, I refuse to handle any small child that isn't safely poppered inside one of these outfits. Besides, they come in such glorious colours. If they made them big enough for a low-slung woman in her prime I'd wear nothing else.

Rompers are a sort of legless, short-sleeved variety of the same thing. With buttons. And elastic. In fact, not the same thing at all. They are still with us after years of proven worth for warmer weather, but thoroughly out of fashion. If you do dress the boy in rompers, especially smocked rompers, don't be surprised if people start to curtsey and call you Ma'am. I suppose princes don't leak.

With the very young there are two things to avoid. One is tight things that have to go over his head. Don't ask me why, but he'll hate it. Perhaps it reminds him of the day he arrived. And the other thing is shoes. Refuse him shoes until he can give you a really good reason, like having an interview for a job.

You can buy shoes for the smallest of babies, and pretty little things they are too. But he doesn't need them. Like you and me, the only reason he'll ever need shoes is that the world is full of broken glass, rusty nails and staggeringly gorgeous fashion. Until he's ready for an encounter with any of these, he is better off barefoot. If you buy him shoes, he will consider it his duty to concentrate hard and lose one of each pair. Always one. He'll find it quite easy to lever the thing off along the edge of the pram and flip it into the hedgerow when you're not looking. The first thing you'll notice, several miles on, will be that he is admiring his foot. And quite right too. Bare and untortured it is a thing of beauty.

Once he becomes a ground dweller there will be a change of emphasis in his wardrobe. Whether he becomes a crawler or a bottom shuffler, his sheer mobility will mean a hard life for his clothes. If I had my time again I would probably go for serviceable shades of grey.

You can get wonderful things for this age group. Paintbox colours, waspish stripes, and witty little details like zip pockets and grandad braces. You could buy a bit of everything. Have him Edwardian in the morning and denim hillbilly in the afternoon. It'll all end up grey.

And do you have a dear little girl who'd look a picture in pink Viyella and white ribbed tights? Did you use to dream of having a daughter? I do understand. Buy her something grey for the time being. Later on she may grow into one of those sort of girls, and it will all look a lot handsomer when she spends less time on the floor.

When a child stands up there is suddenly a lot more of him to dress. For one thing he'll need to be shod. Buying shoes for children is murder. God knows, the shoe shops have done their best. Some of them look like sets for Hansel and Gretel. But it's still murder. Never go on a wet day, and never go when you are overdrawn, pre-menstrual or just full of ordinary violence.

First, you have to sit for an hour while the only Trained Fitter tries endless, identical, black shoes on endless, identical boys called Robert. It is obvious to any eye unwarped by training that the first pair fitted him and that he's only dragging it out until he's seen the Test Match score on the telly in Radio Rentals across the way. Look carefully at Robert's mother. Isn't she the woman from the Anadin advert? Eventually, it will be your turn. Your little lad won't want to get off the rocking horse. After an hour in the saddle he will be getting to like the feel of it. To show just how much he didn't want to get off the rocking horse he will curl his foot into a gross and unmeasureable ball. Trained Fitter is quite accustomed to this sort of behaviour. Her training will have equipped her to deal with it. She will tell you that the shop is about to close and have you thought of a surgical boot.

When your children get too old for the rocking horse and agree to have their feet measured, you'll find that they need a width fitting Z, a width of shoe for which Trained Fitter finds there is no demand. You'll move on to another shop, arrange your wagons in a circle and listen while another Trained Fitter tells you you might get away with a low-cut width Y they happen to have in cherry red. That is when Albert will roll onto the floor, foaming at the mouth with a blue lace-up clutched in his hand. And this is nothing. He's young yet. Once he's at school he'll need a great deal more than blue lace-ups and a pair of Roland Rat slippers. He'll need Trainers and Football Boots and Dancing Pumps. Not to mention Indoor Shoes and Outdoor Shoes. These are a recent development, connected with pale floors, school caretakers and dirt.

The last stage with shoes is the one where they look at everything on display and then tell you that you must be joking. This is easier. You find yourself a seat in a coffee shop and order yourself a cream cake. Then you give each dissenting child a crisp bank note and tell them that you'll be leaving in an hour and will hold them responsible for their own foot deformities.

But to return to the clothes on his back, you'll know from trying to clothe yourself that our shops work on the odd basis that our climate has seasonal variations. In February they sell beachwear for August, and in August all they can offer you is moonboots for February. This is all part of being British. We all know that we live in a place that's cool and wet nearly all the time. Pretending we have summers like Copacabana Beach and winters to vie with Gstaad is no crazier than singing 'Rule Britannia' and believing the words. We all know where the fantasy ends, and that what you need to see you through the year is cardigans and Wellington boots. As long as you hang on to that essential truth, you can equip your children for everything the weather may throw at them.

When you see something on the rail in the shop and it takes your fancy, just consider how it will look with a woolly and wellies, and then make your decision. And never, under any circumstances, buy a sundress. If you take your small daughter anywhere hot enough to wear it, you will need to keep her in the shade until sunset for fear she gets heat stroke. And if you intend summering in Britain, she'll never get to wear it without an Aran jumper and gloves.

If it should turn out fine on the odd day or two, when your children are young, fight your way into one of those shops full of skisuits and refuse to leave until they find a cheap pair of shorts to sell you. Or better still, when things hot up, let your children strip off layer by layer and run around as they are. Your neighbours may already go in for this sort of behaviour themselves, in which case you will have no problems. But they may be horrified. The first time I let a naked toddler play with a bowl of water in her own back garden, I had no idea of the offence I might cause. Hot people in cardigans frowned at me over the fence, and, by the end of the summer, we were surrounded by estate agents' boards. You can hear it all the time on public beaches. Parents holding up enormous towels so that tiny children can wriggle out of their trunks. 'Look sharp, Keith, you don't want everybody seeing your bottom.'

It's a shame, for there's nothing quite like a bit of sunlight and sea breeze to unknot the careworn body, but there we are. I suppose we would never have civilised the rest of the world, if we had all run around without our knickers.

From the toddling stage up to about eleven the matter of what your child actually wears can be kept very simple. Tell him he can only have what you can afford and what has been handed down, and do nothing to encourage him to develop into a walking clotheshorse. Time enough for that later. You *can* have a lengthy discussion with a five year old about whether he'd suit the red trousers better than the green, but I expect you have more urgent things to do with your life.

Your main concern with this age group is getting them to dress themselves competently, showing them where the dirty washing goes before it arrives back clean, and smoothing out any small on-site difficulties. These are nearly always to do with fit. Children hate things that are too tight or too loose or that have scratchy labels or fasteners that won't stay fastened. It's worth while dealing with these hiccups promptly. My rule is – if the problem can be remedied in less than half an hour with standard household equipment, do it. If not, give it away or use it for a floor cloth. There's no point in hanging on to it for the next child in the family. Scratchy jumpers pass into the folk memory, and, if Albert wouldn't wear it, Leonora certainly won't.

Being able to dress yourself is a really useful skill. I know grown men who can't find their own clean socks and a pathetic sight they make. No matter how young your child, the first time he shows any sign of doing the job for himself, encourage him. It will save you hours of tedium if he knows where everything is kept and in what order it goes on. Don't quibble over detail and never discourage by insisting that the vest has to be the right way round. Wearing your tights inside out never hurt anyone. Nor did wearing a pink jersey with an orange skirt and purple body warmer.

You can tell a family of self-dressers at a glance. They look like extras from *Oliver Twist*. If the thought of being seen with this sort of rabble really offends you, or you're certain they'll clash with your Jean Muir, you can try and reduce the number of truly jarring combinations by buying one colour for each child. This is also useful when you find one green sock. It enables you to say with confidence, 'This sock is Albert's.'

But there are families that will even scupper colour coding. Families where children swop clothes and pool resources and where the first up is the best dressed and the last up gets the brown polo neck. They learn a lot about co-operation that way. At least the weakest and sleepiest do. And, if they can co-operate over whose turn it is for the red T-shirt, they can also co-operate over awkward back fastenings and the tying of the school tie. Who wants them to look stage-managed, anyway? Who cares for junior bow ties and screamingly white socks? It would be nice just once in a while, though, wouldn't it?

I have reserved a few rights of veto over my children's clothes. I expect certain standards, if we're visiting a granny. Like only wearing odd socks, if it really can't be helped, and wearing the jersey she knitted because that is only polite. And, if we're going to the doctor's, I forbid any outfit that can't be shed in thirty seconds. I refuse to struggle with bondage wear, when there is a waiting room full of bronchitics needing attention.

Otherwise, I affect not to care. I spent too much of my youth in plastic macs and coats I would grow into to have a lot of time for clothes. And, somehow, even if I tried harder, there would still be some snivelling waif who went blubbing to Granny that her only vest has been used to wipe the dipstick and never been replaced.

Now I should like to say a word about school uniforms. *Hooray*. But what about the cost? And the suppressed individuality of the developing child through a trivial insistence on conformity? Well, they do cost a lot, but what you spend on the uniform you will more than save on time, temper and all the other clothes your child would otherwise wear to school.

Suppressed individuality is something else. It will not harm your child at all. If you have a lot of confused ideas about free-range chickens and the unshackled human spirit, focus your mind on the world your child has to live in. Everything he encounters will be mass-produced. Everywhere he turns, he will sense the deep human fear of being isolated from the tribe. None of us wants to be the last Mohican. Or the last man in Manchester to wear platform shoes.

The sudden urge to be very different doesn't usually strike until the midlife crisis. And, if that's what you're going through, it should be you refusing to wear the bowler hat, not you refusing to let

Albert wear his cap. If you insist on him wearing his Mr T jogging suit for the school photograph by way of an anarchic statement, he will make sure he gets into the back row. Buy him the uniform, correct to the last button, and let him enjoy being the same as everyone else. And another thing. With a uniform there need never ever be an argument on a Thursday morning about whether a velour bomber jacket is a good idea on the day they do gluing.

If you are into a heavy supervision scene, you will consider it reasonable to do the rounds once a day, gathering up dirty clothes and dropping them into the laundry skip. It only takes a moment, and, having done that, it's a simple matter of washing it, ironing it, mending it, shortening it, lengthening it again, and, in your spare time, yomping across Brent Cross to buy replacements. Come on now! Putting the stuff out to be washed is surely the least you can expect of them?

If, when he's ten, you are still sifting through the *Beano*s on his floor sniffing for things that have been worn, how is he ever going to find out that socks don't walk on their own to the washing machine?

I have had moderate success with a method called Leave It and Let Them See What Happens. To be able really to brazen this one out, you need to wait until half term. Then, when there's nothing in his drawer but a pair of swimming trunks and an interesting pebble from Snowdonia, it's no skin off your nose that he has to stay in bed all week. It's a lesson well learned.

He'll remember it for about a fortnight, and then you'll have to repeat the dose or try something stronger. Like an electric cattle prod. But he *can* learn where the dirty laundry goes. He can also learn about washing machines and programme numbers, and where the powder goes in and what happens when you boil a cricket pullover. All this is quite within his grasp. I admit to getting nervous about going that far myself. I think it's because I know exactly how hard I had to work to afford that machine, and I don't want it written off because the lad operating it had his head deep in *A Pictorial History of Snooker*.

But there's nothing to stop them learning to stitch on buttons and name tapes and, eventually, when your nerve is steady, to iron. Start him off on something simple. A king-sized sheet will give him plenty to practise on, if you iron sheets in your house. Introduce him to the iron, tell him about burns, and then leave him to do it with a little help from his personal stereo. One day, when you've gone to Harrogate for your health and the front of his evening shirt needs goffering, he'll thank you for it.

When your children get to about eleven, you will begin to tell the boys from the girls. If it will wear the same pair of jeans for a month, and swear it doesn't matter about the arm hanging out of the anorak as long as the West Bromwich Albion badge is firmly stitched on, it is a boy. If it's not a boy by gender, it is trying to become one by sustained effort. Otherwise, it is a girl, and it will suddenly not be seen dead in any clothes you have chosen. Some girls wait as late as thirteen to get like this, so don't jump the gun. You'll know when the moment has arrived by the way she looks at you. Granny may well suggest kindness through cruelty and a quick dash to Laura Ashley's, but grannies do have some rum ideas – like being able to tell the boys from the girls by which side they button their coats, and the toffs from the peasantry by the shine on their shoes.

Back to gruesome youth. Here is my stratagem. Buy her the things she has to have – the school uniform, the coat and shoes that won't let in the rain, and, if you're a moral coward, one outfit that buttons on the right side and will pass muster with a beady-eyed granny. Then, according to your means, make her a twice-yearly clothes allowance and cut her adrift. No overdrafts and no credit. Like me, you probably have a cupboard full of things you hate and regret. Like me, you know the limitations of a pair of sharp scissors and a tin of Dylon, and you know the whereabouts of the nearest Oxfam shop. And, now our daughters are growing up, it is their turn to learn.

I have road-tested this method on a girl and so far it has worked well. But I confess I have my doubts about it working on a boy. The whole thing about clothes comes much later with lads, and I know plenty of fourteen year olds who would blow the whole lot on Clearasil and fishing tackle and stay in bed when nothing fitted them any more.

Boy or girl, when you reach the clothes allowance stage, it is time to hold your tongue. Whatever they wear will strike you as incredibly ugly and a poor reflection on the way you have dragged them up. Or you will have worn it yourself twenty years ago and be perfectly sure you looked a lot better in it than they do. On both points you must stay mute. Because they're not trying to look like you want them to, they're not interested in what you did in your day and, whatever they wear, it will not matter as long as they remember about kindness to others, the Green Cross Code, and that laundry baskets do not fill themselves.

I knew a man once. I'll call him Ebenezer. His first child had just been born and he told me how appalled he was at the money people spent on toys. 'We're not going to be so foolish,' he said. 'Fran [that was his wife] is going to make lovely things out of grocery cartons.' I believed him. This was a man who made next year's Christmas cards out of last year's Christmas cards and a pair of pinking shears.

We lost touch, what with the price of a second class stamp and all, but I often wonder how he's getting on. His little boy must be about ten by now. I bet Fran had a devil of a time making the BMX out of Persil boxes.

If you're reading this while you wait for your firstborn to arrive, you may feel a lot of sympathy for Ebenezer's philosophy. You may have cast an eye over the lack-lustre generation that has grown up with Masters of the Universe and Barbie's Dream Cottage, and vowed to save your family from treading the same path. Maybe you even own a pair of pinking shears?

Just hang on. Don't get carried away by the thought of all the money you're going to save. Let me explain about frugality in the toy cupboard. You can get away with it for about one year. After that we're talking money.

During the first six months of his life your baby will play with his toes, his fingers, and any part of you he can get a grip on. Then he'll learn to sit unsupported. This is quite a moment. Once you can sit, life gets more varied. You can get dumped by your dad when the phone rings, you can get knocked over by the dog, *and* you can play with things left within your reach. Playthings at this stage can be anything safe. This is the time when a child really is satisfied with a wooden spoon, a saucepan lid and a handful of

dolly pegs. All you need remember is that everything will end up in his mouth, and that he'll get bored if there aren't plenty of things to choose from.

If you are tempted to start buying, you will find as you look around the toy shops that the key features are brightly coloured plastic and versatility of purpose: 'n' is very much in evidence. For instance, a teddy bear phone that rings and is a savings bank. Or a pull-along pony that squeaks with a cart full of alphabet building blocks. Ring'n'save. Squeak'n'build. Not to mention stack'n'pull, sit'n'ride, and of course that perennial favourite, squeal'n'scare, or, as he is better known, Jack in the Box. If you don't buy one for Barnaby, someone else will. When it happens see if you can work out how to take away the squeal without leaving a tell-tale scar.

The things other people buy your young child can be quite important, especially if there are folks in his life like godparents and dowager aunts. Some of them may perform acts of starkly simple giving, like laying down a pipe of port or changing their will. If you move in this sort of circles, this is behaviour to be encouraged. The worst bearers of gifts are those who have never had anything to do with children and may not even have been children themselves. They believe, mistakenly, that they like and understand children. These are the people who find bibs decorated with I AM A LITTLE PERISHER amusing. They are also the ones who buy all those cuddly toys.

Now I'm not a difficult woman. A teddy or two is fine by me. But these people go for overkill, buying their way through the whole animal kingdom. I've seen a cuddly banana. To be scrupulously honest, we've got a cuddly banana. It is upstairs, unloved, even as I write. Some people will buy anything. I swear that, if someone marketed fur fabric tape worms, godfathers and maiden aunts would queue up to buy them. Worse still, they are seduced by size. They figure that if their nephew is happy with a twelve-inch teddy, he'll be delirious with a five-footer. They are wrong. Five-foot teddies are for big girls who never want to grow up. Smaller teddies are for children old enough to need a friend when the going gets tough. I know a ten-year old, man enough to have been abseiling *and* watched very old Vincent Price films all on his own, who still likes to confide in a Pink Panther.

You might be tempted by a mobile. We all have our moments. I'm not sure how this terrible foreign idea came to us, but I'd guess that, if the trail has not gone cold, it would lead us to Sweden.

I spent the first months of my life looking at cream distemper and brown bakelite electrical arrangements. And, unless you are a very young parent indeed, so did you. There may have been the occasional foray into exotica, like a morning in the pram under a blossom-laden bough, or a quick push home under the stars when my parents had been out visiting, but I can safely say I was never subjected to a mobile.

Mobiles are part of the idea that a child will reward your non-stop stimulation during his early years by turning into a genius. First, let's suppose that this is true. Do you want a genius? Are you sure? Are you planning to have other children? And how many geniuses would you say you could cope with? Second, let's suppose that stimulating a child all the time is going to do no such thing. Let's suppose it's going to do the same to them as it would do to you and me – make them tired and irritable. Is it any wonder that young people today look so jaded? They've been got at since the first day they rolled onto their backs and looked up. Bring back cream distemper, that's my advice. And an hour under the lilac bush, if it turns out fine. All right. I'd say wind chimes were just about allowable. Just about.

But if you want to, in that first year you can get away with buying nothing. If you do buy something, it will afford you a lot more satisfaction than it will your child and he will be more than contented with an empty squash bottle, the cat and your face.

During his second year, several things will happen to your baby. He will become highly mobile and he'll start to display likes and dislikes without being articulate enough to justify the way he feels. That's what all the screaming will be about. Every day the possibilities will increase and this will be reflected in the gulf between what he wants to do and what you, as his elder and better, can allow.

Once he can get about, the world starts to look like a giant Asda Warehouse. He'd quite happily spend the whole day pulling things on top of himself, poking things into electric sockets, and seeing how many things bounce. Toys for this age group are therefore designed to distract him from his great drive to self-destruct. There's a catch phrase you may have heard – the Terrible Twos. It's true. The reason he'll be terrible is that you will have given him a Wheel'n'Wings Camper that's a pickup that's a dumper that's a jet plane, and what he will really want to do is pick all the wallpaper off the wall behind your chair and eat the telephone cable. Remember this before you go shopping. Two year olds are as difficult as goats to divert from their mission to eat and destroy.

One of the few activities you will be able to interest him in is pushing. Any child that has learned to walk will enjoy pushing something around on wheels. It can be a pram, a wheelbarrow, or just an ordinary old truck. Whatever it is he'll put everything in it, including himself, and spend hours running it into legs. Chippendale and otherwise. You should get at least one of these push'n'bash outfits. The mathematics of them works out like this. If you have one more of them than the total number of children normally resident, one of the push'n'bash outfits will stand ignored and neglected until the day some kind visiting child takes pity on it and lifts his hand to wipe away the dust. At that moment every other child in the garden will desire it more than anything else in the world and will lie down and hold his breath until he gets it. This is as predicted by Bugger's Law of Inverse Proportions of Availability and Value.

For this age group there are also toys meant to keep him out of your tool box and out of your hair. These are the Little Helpers. You can get ironing boards, tea sets, little driver dashboards, construction tool sets and even a moulded party kitchen comprising a four-burner range with clicking knobs, large sink, drop-leaf table, spice rack and towel rail – so what more could a boy ask for?

The trouble with all these things is that they are only pretend. And what your average two year old really wants is to get right in there, with the greasy saucepans and the frayed flex and the blunted scissors you're keeping in case you're ever silly enough to try and lay another carpet yourself. If you must have a Little Helper, buy a tea set. It is infinitely versatile and, if in your garden you have a few square yards laid to mud, it will be terrifically good play value, indoors and out.

Versatility is an important feature. With most toys it is illusory. A robot that is a blackboard, a shape-sorter and a counting frame is essentially a robot that's a blackboard that's . . . If it can be used as an emergency transmitter when you're playing Jaws, or to stand on when you want to reach something interesting on a high shelf, *then* it's versatile.

A good rule of thumb is this. If it's made of brightly coloured moulded plastic and is advertised as being educational and multipurpose, then it probably isn't. You shouldn't worry. Given the chance your child will show you the true meaning of multi-purpose. Would *you* have thought of making a trampoline on a very wet lawn with every pillow and cushion in the house and asking an adult *afterwards*? Neither would I. But it was a genuinely multi-purpose occasion. We learned about trampolines and wetness and the loudness of angry voices. We also explored the sensitive issue of corporal punishment. And no toy shops were involved.

This is also the time when you become aware that what your child is seen with will reflect upon you. You won't want people thinking you're not a serious-minded parent. Are you eager to avoid sexual and racial stereotyping? Are you into good design? Sturdy pieces of smooth, naturally coloured wood that will last forever? So was I. One of the reasons they will last forever is that Barnaby will leg it over the fence every afternoon to play with Loretta's plastic Get Along Gang in next door's garden. I'm saving all our wooden toys for the grandchildren.

If you do buy him a handcarved Noah's Ark, he will immediately become inseparable from something cheap and vulgar that surfaced in the church bazaar bran tub. He will insist on taking it everywhere with him, especially to birthday parties held for the Junior Terence Conran Crowd, and he will refuse to lose it on a bus or a train. You must either swallow your humiliation until the phase has passed, or try to lose the thing for him. But don't try shaking it off at the J T Cs' because they will remember exactly whom it belongs to and return it to you in a plain brown package as soon as the post office is open.

And books. You'll be wanting to ensure that Barnaby develops a love of good books. Maybe you have already selected a few of the very best. Books with clear, attractive illustrations and no-nonsense texts. Books like *Sam and Daddy Iron a Shirt*. I hope you enjoy them. Your child will prefer something tacky, sexist and full of bunnies. He will have a particular favourite. He'll look at it until the covers drop off and, every time he does, he'll ask you whether the wolf can eat him and why has the girl got red shoes.

These sorts of books are easy to acquire. They just sort of arrive in bags of things people think you may be glad of. Little knitted jackets

with matted sleeves, an electric bottle-warmer without a plug, and books like *Jimbly Wimbly's Woodland Friends*. Or *Fluffy and Wuffy Go To The Seaside*, first published in 1957 and not much improved in the meanwhile. Relax. A brush with Enid Blyton won't mark them for life. It's not a good start but it need not mean that your child will never finish *War and Peace*. After all, what's your excuse?

You must be just about into your third year by now. Doesn't time fly? This is the year your child can start to discover the outdoors. The year he really finds his voice and his muscles, and if you don't want him shinning up your velvet drapes and running along the top of your Chesterfield, I recommend you invest in something to stretch his capabilities outside.

I'll tell you first what you don't want. You don't want anything that has to be searched for in the garden shed, assembled, and checked for safety by a member of the government inspectorate every time someone wants to use it. We're talking permanent here. We're talking nuts, bolts and concrete, and goodbye to a little bit of garden. Get a swing, or a climbing frame or a slide. If you've got the space and the money, get all three. And get them properly installed. It will keep him amused for years.

The disadvantage is that the word will get round very quickly and you'll be plagued by every child in the neighbourhood from daybreak until the street lights come on. The same thing will happen if you have a sandpit. Don't have a sandpit. Even if you have it fitted with a cover that has a hair-trigger siren and can deliver a 240 volt shock, every dog, cat and armadillo in the county will get into it and use it as a toilet. Stay with some basic, dependable playground equipment and discourage unwanted visitors by looking very fierce and grumpy.

Another worthwhile but seasonal thing is a tent. I don't mean one of those fabric playhouses that you throw over a plastic frame, hoping it won't blow away before the toddlers have squeezed inside it. I mean a proper tent. Give them a tent, a tea set and a couple of push-along trucks and you won't hear from them all day.

And the best thing of all? A tree. Not the Japanese Weeping Cherry you planted last month. A proper tree that's older than you are. You may need to move house for this one. What you want is a tree that's large enough and sound enough to be played on. A rope ladder is one good thing. An old car tyre on a rope is another. And a tree house is *Absolutely Ace*. I'd say it was worth a Fortress of Mystery and Power, a radio-controlled A-team van, a Crystal Barbie Motor Home, and then some.

Other outdoor toys, like motorbikes and tricycles, are annoying but essential. You need one per child at all times, otherwise the child with the strongest elbows always gets the ride and all the others lie down in his path and scream. I've seen more bloodshed over things on wheels than I've seen over anything else in the toy box.

Of course, even with a well-equipped adventure playground outside the kitchen window, he'll want to come in from time to time, to change his shirt and see how the old folks are getting along. When he does come in, if he's allowed to watch television, there's something you should be warned of. From October until December 24th restrict him to the channels that don't carry adverts. If you have any doubts about the power of advertising, just try an hour of commercial television in the run-up to Christmas and notice how every jingle is instantly memorised and every toy is immediately and desperately longed for.

Once your child has gone beyond the stage of trying to swallow or push up his nose anything smaller than a football the world of toys will be yours for the having. A great abyss filled with overpriced, under-engineered tawdry tat will open beneath you. I advise you to concentrate on falling into it with care and dignity, rather than pretend that you're not going to fall at all.

I'll give you a quick guided tour of this Grotto of Nightmares. After that, you'll have plenty of time to explore on your own. You'll be here for ten years at least. And beyond it there are Compact Disc Stack Systems, teenage pregnancies and real motorbikes. So don't hurry.

The first thing to beware of is the '-ettes'. You've weathered the 'n's. Now it's the '-ettes'. Typewriter-ettes, sewing machine-ettes and carpentry set-ettes are money down the drain. If your child is sufficiently co-ordinated and interested to want to type, sew or hammer, you'd be better off parking him with an expert and kindly adult for the odd afternoon and letting him have a go with the real tools. '-Ettes' raise a child's expectations unreasonably and leave him frustrated when he's stitched his fingers to the material and failed to make you the ballgown he promised.

Then there are the mini-industries. You will get caught up by one of them. The only question is which one? For each new character that is created there will be a whole pile of accessories for you to buy. Moneymad Melinda or Warlock the Weirdo, or whoever you end up with, are really into consumer durables.

For Melinda you might buy a play patio with sliding patio doors, a dream kitchen (Melinda significantly not included in this package) or a home gymnasium with vanity area and matching man with fully poseable body. Go for Warlock and you'll be no less spoilt for choice. Quite apart from the warrior assault vehicles, subterranean sidewinders, and evil mountain stronghold made of evil painted cardboard, there will be a board game, a bedside mat, a bedside mat that makes into a board game and a Weirdo Warlord toothbrushing timer'n'toothbrush. See! No sooner have you dodged the '-ettes' than the 'n's have crept up on you again.

These inventors are really on to something. They know that with a little encouragement children can be as acquisitive and gullible as adults. Dream up a character and he'll sell anything for you: anything from a lunchbox to a six-pack of party hats. You are listening to a woman who fought a rearguard action against Sindy for years. I know normal, likeable people who can't get into their houses for Sindy's horse, Sindy's dog, her barbecue and pool set and boxes full of her leisure wear. No one leaves the Grotto of Nightmares empty handed. You too will pass this way.

But there are still plenty of things that are worth buying. Paints and paper are inexhaustibly good. For drawing on skin, chair covers and table legs, felt-tip pens are best. And face paints are wizard. Despite what any label says they will only wash off with a lot of soap and a stiff nailbrush, but they are great fun to put on.

Modelling materials are worth having as well. I don't mean false eyelashes. I mean the stuff you can roll out into very long worms. Choose one that doesn't smell nasty and try to get it in a colour that tones with your carpet. You can actually make some yourself with ordinary household ingredients. I think life is too short for this lark but, if you must know, you need about a pound of plain flour, a fist full of table salt, a splodge of colour, either food colouring or coloured powder paint, and enough cheap cooking oil to mix it to a modelling consistency. Wrapped in clingfilm in the fridge, this will keep for quite a while before it starts to smell unhealthy.

Dolls are another must. Even if you have five sons, you must have dolls. It doesn't matter how battered and ugly they are. If they come with clothes, that's fine. They will all end up the same way – naked and minus one leg. The ones that perform with the aid of batteries are not worth having. They won't get played with until they've gone through the initiation ceremony that removes their batteries, their clothes and their right leg. When they start to look like the others, they will become loved and trodden on.

Dolls' houses, on the other hand, like train sets, snooker tables and model farms, are best kept at Granny's. That way *she* can keep track of all the little bits and pieces that make the toy worthwhile, and the opportunities to play with it will be so rare that it will always be deeply treasured and fondly remembered.

How do you feel about guns? No child of mine was ever going to have one. When a child of mine first saw one, she wanted it so much she was prepared to kill to get her hands on it. In the end, I allowed a gun or two into the house. And bows and arrows and swords. I even went to Woolworth's to buy caps. You may think I've been unnecessarily flabby on this issue, but I thought I'd leave them to grow into their own moral postures. Eventually, the guns sank to the bottom of the toy box, along with the doll's leg and the torchless battery.

With what's left of your budget I'd go for board games, jigsaws and dressing-up clothes by the sackful. You can't have too many pairs of high heeled shoes, preferably glittery party shoes. Nurse's outfits and Spiderman suits are all well and good, but you really cannot beat a bag full of old hats, jewel-encrusted shoes and Batman cloaks. A tea set, a gobbet of plasticine stuck to the bottom of a silver shoe and a cloak are what a four year old means by the word *Heaven*.

And a final word. Don't worry too much about those Eezy-kleen Storage Units. By all means, make them bundle everything away at bedtime. But the randomness of up-ending a box the next morning and seeing what comes out on top is one of life's richer pleasures. That way, on the day Barnaby finds the roller skate, the Batman cloak can take a well-earned rest.

8   *The Amateurs*

Time was when playgroups would have had no takers. Time was when a mother spent her time darning and mangling and making pegged rugs, and, even if there had been such a thing as Activities for the pre-school child, she would never have had time to get along there.

I know a few survivors from those hard times. And their children. Pleasant, middle-aged people who never got to join the Humpty Dumpty Club. I've often wondered what the pre-school playgroup would have done for them.

We are told that prudent use of those early years will show dramatically later in life. That the child who has attended a nursery school, or even a humble Toddler Group, will be better equipped, intellectually and socially, for the experience of school. We are told. And, as none of us wants our children doomed to a life of dumb ineptitude, we do all we can to leg them up to the top of the heap. We hear stories about the semi-literate hordes that schools belch out each July, and they make us reach for the Alphabet Bricks. We get ourselves down to the Community Centre and enrol Randolph for anything that's on offer. If there are children down there of an afternoon, mugging up on Elements of Euclidian Geometry, we don't want anyone from our family getting left behind, do we?

You may have other reasons for getting his name on to that register. You may be feeling lonely, or bored. You may rightly feel that you need to get out and talk to people. Or you may be too chicken to say No to the hardselling neighbour who knocks on your door to drum up a bit of business for the local playgroup. These are all understandable and forgivable reasons for getting involved. But, if you think that by turning out in all weathers to do communal footpainting, you are safeguarding Randolph's place in the First Division of life, you are very mistaken. Let me tell you what really goes on at these places.

The first thing you qualify for is a Mother and Toddler Group. These are organised by enterprising mothers with young children, and if there isn't one in your area and you wish there was, you can start one. Being involved in the setting up of one of these groups can be a marvellous thing. It will get you talking to other people, it will get you out of the house, and it will require all the skills of diplomacy and organisation that you can muster.

The one thing Mother and Toddler Groups are not for is toddlers. If you've got one you can take him along. In fact you don't even have to wait until he's a bona fide toddler. He can go when he's a month old, if that's what you need, but you must never forget what a disagreeable view of society you will be giving him, and at such a tender age.

At a Mother and Toddler Group there will be chairs for the mothers to sit on, a stack of toys for the toddlers, and drinks and biscuits halfway through the session. There will also be a lot of noise. You may be so intoxicated by all that human contact that you don't notice you have a headache, but Randolph will notice that he has one. Added to which, his nervous system will be raw and sparky from drinking cheap orange juice and meeting a roomful of chaps who are as graceless as he is.

This is a Mothers' Meeting trading under a misleading name. I use the word Mother in the loosest sense. If you are a father, you can just as easily join. For the first six months you will be treated charily, but eventually they'll thaw out enough to compare varicose veins in front of you and, before you know where you are, they'll have you making a Wendy House.

But we are forgetting the suffering masses. Toddlers don't talk to each other and they don't play with each other. They are far too young for conversation or co-operation. They grab and yell and hurtle and bite and urinate and worse. They do it all afternoon, and their mothers talk, oblivious to everything. If a chap doesn't care for what's going on, the only course open to him is to crawl under his mother's chair and suck his thumb, very hard.

These groups are especially popular with the mothers of only children. 'I want him to meet other children and learn to share,' they explain.

He will certainly meet other children. He will find that, like him, they have runny noses, baggy trousers and are none too steady on their pins. In every other respect they might as well come from Mars. They smell different, they use a different system of grunts, and they plainly do not understand that when a chap has hold of a pushalong tinkletonk, he wants to hang on to it.

He will not learn to share. He'll learn that some toddlers are bigger than others and get what they want at everyone else's expense. This may be a useful lesson in life, but it has nothing at all to do with sharing.

Toddlers are whimsical creatures. Given a room full of variety they will career from one thing to another, wanting everything and sticking at nothing. Given solitude they will sit all afternoon with one toy, absorbed in the monotonous repetition of piling up the bricks and knocking them down again. After a spell on his own like this, he will be tranquil and satisfied, in a toddley sort of way. But after an afternoon fighting for his life at Mother and Toddlers, he will be overwrought, insecure and fit only for a quick tea and bed.

I'm not saying you shouldn't go. The benefits to you may outweigh the effects on him. I can remember how supportive and enervating the company of other parents can be. But I learned it was better to keep the group small. No more than four adults and attached children at a time. I found that it all jangled less when I reduced it to a domestic scale, and I found I enjoyed it all a lot more when I stopped expecting to like everyone else's children and settled for putting up with them.

When your child gets to about three he will be eligible for something more ambitious. A nursery school, or a playgroup.

A nursery school is a professional or semi-professional set up. It will be headed by someone who has to balance the books, and it will cost you accordingly. There will be permanent accommodation, with cloakroom pegs and classes that have jolly names like The Lions and The Elephants. If you send your child to one of these places for a year or two before he starts school, the real thing will then hold no surprises for him. He'll arrive there knowing quite a lot of playground lore. He'll also know how to write his name and say his numbers. He'll have made egg-carton alligators, mustard and cress gardens, and learned to tie his shoe laces, and the only problem I can see is that he will spend his first two years at school hanging around while everyone else catches up. It's a bit like letting him learn to drive in a Porsche and buying him a Morris Minor as soon as he's passed his test.

Nursery schools demand quite a lot of their children and, although there is something impressive about four year olds hanging their painting aprons on the right peg and walking in an obedient crocodile to the park, there is also something about it that makes me uneasy. There are all sorts of things four year olds like to do. Making a den with the cushions off the three-piece suite; sleeping all afternoon; or sitting on a high stool watching someone make pastry and asking whether the sky is bigger than a lorry and why do some ladies have a hairy face. Me and my kids didn't get to make egg-box alligators until we were five. I just hope we turn out all right in the end.

A playgroup is not a lot like a nursery school. Like the Toddler Group it owes its existence to the energy of a few dedicated parents, and, like any self-funding, self-promoting group, it is always eager for new blood. If there is a playgroup in your area and your children are the right age for it you will find it difficult not to join. If you don't, the word will get round that you are members of an obscure religious sect, or the victims of chronic impetigo. And, if you do join, in no time at all you will get sucked in.

You cannot pay your dues and then expect merely to consume what the group has to offer. A playgroup is a labour-intensive microcosm. Everything it owns and everything it achieves comes from its own efforts and it cannot afford to support drones. You must be prepared to roll up your sleeves and be a worker. There is only one thing a playgroup can have too many of, and that is queens. There should really only be one.

You'll spot the Queen Bee easily the first time you cart young Randolph along to the Scout hut. She will have a high, excited voice, a pencil behind her ear and a spare pair of children's knickers somewhere about her person. Queen bees are powerful women. They have strong views about children and even stronger views about parents. The average playgroup only has room for one of these people at a time: one queen and one heir presumptive in case she goes down with laryngitis. I've seen usurper queens come buzzing in, full of Montessori correspondence courses, and I've seen them stung into silence. Playgroups are very political.

If you get the lad's name down in time, he should be able to start when he's three or three and a half. If there's a long waiting list, don't panic. It isn't Charterhouse. I'd say starting at four was quite soon enough.

The first day you go, Randolph will give you immediate feedback about his gut reaction. He will either run in and jump into the sandpit without stopping to unzip his anorak, or he will leap into your arms and stay there like a sobbing barnacle until you take him home.

If he does the first thing, you will be asked if you would like to stay, and how many sugars do you take in your coffee? If he does the second thing, he will be levered off you by Queen Bee, no anaesthetics used, and you will be told to go away for a couple of hours to somewhere you won't be able to hear his cries. I've gone over this again and again in my mind. I'm sure I've got it the right way round.

The idea is to get him to the anorak in the sandpit stage as soon as possible. Because children have to learn. Well, so they do. What I can never understand is why they have to learn that when they're happy and busy their mother sticks around queering their pitch, and when they're frightened and miserable she runs away to Dickins & Jones. Maybe it was never explained to me properly.

If Randolph is bored at home, playgroup is the very place for him. Even the most modest of groups will have an astounding range of activities to offer him. There will be a climbing frame, bikes and prams, a playhouse, a book corner, a painting table, toy cars, and as many dressing-up clothes as a chap could dream of. And, on top of all this, there will usually be some special activities going on as well. Possibly something seasonal at the pasting table. Or a brave father who has brought along his guitar and his Ralph McTell songbook.

If you stay for the whole session, either because you're new and they want to find out all about you, or because your name has come to the top of the helpers' rota, special activities are where you are most likely to get posted. You'll be given twenty sheets of orange paper and a black marker pen and asked to do something simple but effective for Hallowe'en. Or to fill a fifteen-minute gap in the morning with a display of finger rhymes.

As a helper mother, what you will find is this. Some children go to playgroup to spread lots of paste on pieces of paper. Some go to jump off the top of the climbing frame. Some always pedal a bike very fast and go Vroooooom, some always wear an old net curtain and wet themselves rather than leave their dolls' pram unattended. And there is always a big boy called Andrew. You'll usually find him sitting in a very small pedal car.

One of your responsibilities as helper mother will be to try and persuade the bike riders to paste Hallowe'en pictures, and the paste addicts to go and stretch their legs for a while. Another will be to say, 'No,' in a chummy sort of way every time Andrew smashes into you and says, 'You Kevin's Mummy?'

You will *not* be expected to try and counsel the child who is showing signs of serious emotional disturbance in the toilets. That will be a job for Queen Bee, because she will have been on a course and know about these things. And you will not be expected to break the news of head lice to anxious waiting parents. That too is a job for an expert.

Halfway through the morning there'll be a break for drinks and biscuits. Time for a breather, you might think. Time to slip out the

back for a Park Drive and a private pee. Not so. Time instead for you to discover what acts of unbridled obscenity the average four year old can perform with a beaker of milk and a Rich Tea Finger. Time to watch Andrew arm-wrestle everyone for their rations without even getting out of the pedal car. And, before you know where you are, it's time to get back to all those activities. The pasters paste on, the bikers bike, and at Queen Bee's suggestion you will sit on a very small chair and play Picture Dominoes with yourself. You'll feel like you've set up a Venereal Disease Information Stand at the Ideal Home Exhibition.

At the end of the session there will be a Quiet Time. It gives the workers time to put everything away and, as the parents arrive to collect their children, it gives an impression of cosy good order. There will be a story. It's not an easy thing to tell a story to twenty children who want their dinner. Some of them will have their coats and hats on already, and the bikers will still be lapping the room, even though their bikes have been put away. I speak from bitter experience. I know the difficulties a woman encounters when she tries to tell the story of the Enormous Turnip to a circle of children who have paired off to bite each other. Her load is not lightened by persons in dungarees sweeping up lentils at close quarters and hissing, 'Get them to do the noises!' I should know. Only my own daughter listened politely, and even she had one eye on the clock.

The mothers arrive then. And in these days of lowered job security, quite a lot of fathers. They bundle the pasty pictures and the wet knickers into their bags and they are gone. But that isn't the end of the matter. There's a lot more to a playgroup than meets the eye. Funds to raise, outings to organise, activities to invent, and committees to convene. The two hours, three mornings a week, that you have seen are the tip of the proverbial iceberg. Once you're into playgroups your life will change. You will never have an idle moment. No sooner will you have ferried jumble in your hatchback than there will be a cake stall to be filled. There can be no better apprenticeship for belonging to that other fount of frenzied self-help, a Parent Teacher Association.

Something else will happen to you as well. Suddenly you will be quite unable to throw anything away. You'll hang on to milk bottle tops and empty roll-on deodorants and have only the vaguest of plans for them. Everything that you once thought of as household rubbish will seem to hold the promise of a fulfilling experience for the pre-school child. This type of behaviour can run out of control very fast. Thriftiness and providence may be no more than a step away from mania. You will need watching carefully. Your family may think you are fine, not realising that you have become a secret hoarder of toilet roll tubes. When someone uncovers a cache of empty yogurt pots while they're searching for their badminton racket, they may be alerted by your frantic denials. But they may not. If you have kept the polystyrene packing that came with your deep fat fryer and you are sure it's going to come in handy for something, I must tell you that yours is a critical case and you must get help at once. You should take a cold bath while the emergency services clear your home of pieces of string and dried sunflower seeds, and get your doctor to give you a certificate that says you need a long rest from collage.

Playgroup will also rope you in for the big occasions. The Christmas Party. The Outing. The Pancake Race.

The Christmas party is mainly jelly and anguish. Some of the children will run and hide as soon as Father Christmas puts his head round the door, but most of them will know exactly whose grandad it is and be interested only in ripping the wrapping paper off their Blackberry Farm story book and getting back to the fizzy pop.

Outings are harder still. Two adults per child *and* eyes in the back of your head wouldn't feel like it was enough. If you go to the fire station, you'll be worried about all those moving parts. If you go to the park, there will be moving parts and space to get lost in. And, if you go to a farm there will be moving parts, space to get lost in *and* at least two muddy boots to each child. When you get back to base, the children will be asked to draw a picture of something they saw at the farm, while you adults try to pair up the wellies. There will be an odd Wellington, twelve drawings of space rockets, four of AN HOUSE and one of an elephant. And Andrew will have made his piece of paper into a pedal car.

Then there will come the day when someone escapes. If you are there when it happens it will be all hands to the pump. In my playgroup days we had plenty who threatened to do it, but only one with the brains and the muscle to carry it off. We looked everywhere for him. Even in a small box of Christmas decorations that hadn't been down off the shelf for eight months. Queen Bee went very pale and said she'd stay behind to make a pot of strong tea while we workers ransacked the streets for one little boy. It was a salutary lesson in how far a four year old can get without his coat or his hat or a single responsible adult wondering what he was doing all on his own in a town. We found him at his grandad's. He said he didn't like playgroup and that he'd rather help his grandad do some hammering. And that brings me to the strange ideas playgroups have about children.

The first is that children should be doing something all the time. The second is that there should be a purpose to everything they do. And the third is that it takes an adult, in constant attendance with a Pritt stick, to keep them on course.

I must remind you what a recent development childhood is. For centuries there was nothing more than an awkward pause between the day he learned to walk and the day he was privileged to start work as a table leg up at The Big House. That short time was filled with the simplest of activities. Hopscotch. Five Stones. Knocking on people's doors and running away. Christmas was an orange and a peg doll. Your birthday was a new pair of boots. And the main thing you learned was when to duck. Childhood was the briefest of interludes, conducted in grim schoolrooms and out in the street. Everyone was relieved when it was over and the child was old enough to crawl down a coal mine or fight for his country.

There were no Wipe Clean Counting Cards or Play and Learn Maracas, and yet people still managed to grow up to be engineers and musicians. Childhood accustomed them to the drudgery and loneliness that accompany all personal achievement. When all you have in the world is a slice of bread and dripping and an old pram wheel, and your mother is too busy scrubbing the front step to speak a civil word to you, what do you do? You draw upon other resources, that's what. You find three other lads with old pram wheels and beg an orange box off the man at the corner shop. Then you burn the box for warmth and spend the day discussing why none of your mothers ever speaks to you and why people keep giving you old pram wheels.

But today's parent won't settle for that. The child would but the parent won't let him. The world is alive with Build As You Go Activity Packs and hearty TV presenters. Everywhere there are opportunities to realise Randolph's full potential and get him through Common Entrance.

Twenty years ago, if someone had been so avant garde as to show you a bag of haricot beans, you would probably have thought first of how uncomfortably close foreignness seemed to be getting, and second, maybe, of cooking them. Today you would also consider whether you should use them to show Randolph how to count, or donate them straight to playgroup so everyone can try making a simple musical instrument. My children graduated from playgroup a long time ago but I still have difficulty parting with empty cotton reels. It is a sickness, and our children don't need or ask for any of it.

I was once involved with a playgroup that decided it should have a woodwork table. It was really nice. A little table with odds and ends of wood, and hammers and nails and a neat little saw – for three and four year olds. I probably don't need to tell you what happened, but I will. No one actually lost an eye, but it was a close run thing. The most noteworthy point was that no one made anything. How could they? They weren't strong enough, or co-ordinated enough, and being modern children they were all so hooked on instant results that they were bound to get more gratification out of chasing each other with the hammers and the bradawl than they ever could out of wonky sawing. The person who got the most out of the venture was the woman who had dreamed it up. She'd had a marvellous time buying all the bits and pieces. And I had quite a bit of fun with it myself. But my three year old would sooner have been at home, doing what three year olds like best. Sitting in a grocery carton all morning and letting it be different things. Or sitting on someone's lap with your thumb and your Best Blanket and watching the 2.30 from Kempton Park.

Never forget that wherever ten or twenty young children are gathered together with eager adults and equipment that carries the kite-mark of good design, you have an unnatural situation. Never forget that discovery of the pre-school child has not filled the world with bright, socially adroit young things. The world is about the same as it was before, except that there are a few more fifteen year olds who can't add up.

If your home is at the pinnacle of automated perfection and you are going quietly round the bend for want of adult company, a playgroup may be the very thing you need. But consider first whether it is fair on the child. While you are happily cutting out thirty stand-up Easter chickens and comparing sandwich toasters with Queen Bee, he will be risking broken teeth, loss of concentration and, after his first encounter with Andrew, a deep and abiding mistrust of the whole human race.

Sooner or later you will be obliged to get your child an education.
It may be a matter of careful planning from the very day he was
born, or simply a case of finding the nearest school and pushing
him in through the gate. You may want your child to go to your
own old school. This is a very sensible way to spend your money,
if you have any. There can be no better way of ensuring that he
grows up with exactly the same phobias and prejudices you did.
Think of the arguments this will save when he gets older.

If he comes home bleating about the bullying and the thrashing,
as a survivor of the system you will be the perfect judge of whether
he's getting enough. You'll understand the slang, you'll know
which boys are of ancient enough stock to be worth cultivating,
and you may even know some of the schoolmasters. I'd say it was
terrifically good value for money – if you've got it. If you haven't,
you must face up to the fact that your child will grow up without
useful friends or sado-masochistic sexual fantasies. He'll never get
to be President of the Oxford Union, and it will take him years to
get into the Freemasons. So, if you find that prospect hard to
endure, isn't it about time you thought on and put a bob or two
by?

You can look for what you think is a good state school and then
move house to be in the right catchment area. This is a dangerous
sport. Schools go downhill very fast and climb back very slowly.
What seemed like a prudent move when Geoffrey was four can
hang round your neck like an albatross when the school hits the
skids and you can't *give* houses away down your street.

If you're conservation minded, you can support a threatened
village school, but you will spend a lot of time writing letters. The
idea of this is to make your MP gibber at the sight of Royal Mail

vans and help you feel less impotent in the face of bureaucracy and harsh economics.

Or you can spend your money on petrol instead of postage stamps and drive your children miles across county boundaries to a good school, whatever that may be.

If I had to choose one feature to insist upon in a school, it would be quietness. Most modern schools are built to an open plan design, and most modern children are built to an open mouth design. This is a blueprint for noise. And, if there is incessant noise, the people living in the middle of it will get so used to it they won't notice how bad it is or how bad tempered it's making them. I would support any school that shows children that you can be happy and quiet, all at the same time.

If your oldest child isn't at school yet, you may be thinking that, when it happens, it will sever forever the intimate relationship between you. This painful prospect may be softened by another thought. That you will gain a measure of freedom you've not had since he was born. That was what we all thought. We were wrong.

For a start we are talking about a relationship that cannot be severed. It is made of indestructible elastic. Dead or alive you are his parent for the duration, and though school may stretch things further than they've ever had to reach before, it will all come twanging back to you at the most surprising moments. He'll still love you as much and miss you a lot, and when he gets home he'll show you how much he's missed you by watching TV when you speak to him and kissing you passionately just as his fish fingers burst into flames.

As for freedom, you'll have less of it, not more. You'll have a schedule to work to – school hours, school holidays, and every evening, when school is out, there will be something that has to be done before nine o'clock the next morning. The days of sleeping late, eating fruit cake for breakfast and reading Scott Fitzgerald while he plays in the bath are over for ever. Get up, pull a comb through your hair and splash a bit of Lifebuoy round your armpits. From here on in you are on parade and the school gate is no place for the habits of a lifetime.

If you are invited to take him to school for half a day before he gets properly blooded, you should accept. It is very bad form to have a prior engagement, and, anyway, it will do you good to sit on one of those little bum-numbing chairs and discover there are more hopeless cases than yours. There you were worrying that Geoffrey can't always manage his own shoe laces, and you've already spotted a girl who doesn't know her own name, and two children of indeterminate sex who do not understand the meaning of the word No.

You'll be feeling better already. This is a good moment to meet Geoffrey's teacher. I'll call her Mrs Robinson. In my experience that's nearly always what her name is.

You'll like Mrs Robinson. For the time being. As she talks to you, slowly and reassuringly about Breakthrough to Literacy and head lice you will find it hard to believe that you will ever call her That Bloody Woman. But you will.

Two things will not have changed since you were at school. One will be the wonderful sound of children singing. And the other will be the smell of Mrs Robinson. I used to think it was chalk, but it isn't. It's plimsolls and wax crayons, and that mat they all sit on when it's Quiet Time. I don't suppose any amount of shampoo gets a smell like that out of your hair.

Anyway, this pleasant woman who smells of plimsolls will tell you a thing or two. She'll tell you that absolutely everything must have a name tape stitched to it, and just as you drift off into a little reverie about what sort of people name-tape knickers she'll wake you up to tell you she really does mean *everything*.

She'll mention punctuality, parental co-operation and infectious diseases, but she won't give the children a glance. They will be elsewhere giving a Classroom Helper the blitzkrieg treatment, so that Mrs Robinson can weigh you up and note how you rate on the scale of reprehensible sloppiness. When she's licked you into shape, she will be ready to make a start on Geoffrey.

School doesn't come as a shock to many children these days. Most of them have had sight of something worse, like a nursery or a playgroup, long before the age of five. This means a lot less heartache on the first day of a new intake. A few will lie down in the cloakroom and weep. One or two of their children may lie down and join them, but mostly it's a very stoic occasion. Not like the old days. I can remember my mother's face pressed against the classroom window. I can even remember what she was wearing, and that was 1952. There was much gnashing of teeth and rending of garments by everyone that day. Nowadays you just won't get away with that sort of behaviour. You'll be expected to stand well back, out of sight of the initiates, comparing squash rackets with all the other newly free.

On his first proper day at school the boy will be looking pretty snappy. Buttoned up, tucked in, with his cowlick glued into submission and his *Tom and Jerry* lunchbox all shiny and new. The next time you'll see him will be only six hours later.

You'll have been at home scrubbing round the cup handles with an old toothbrush because suddenly you don't feel like studying for a new career. You'll have eaten pickled onions straight from the jar, watched a Dirk Bogarde film in black and white, and kept checking that the clock hadn't stopped. And you'll have got yourself up to the school gate in good time.

There will be other women who are there half an hour early as well. You'll start up a series of aimless conversations on anything domestic and uncontroversial. Over the next few years you're going to get to know these women. Some days they will be the only adults you speak to apart from a faintly familiar man who rings for room service in the middle of the evening. You'll learn their names and which are their children. Later, some of the reserve will disappear and they'll tell you how to deep-freeze pancakes and the best thing for biro on a school tie. But they will never tell you anything interesting. Like how they make themselves carry on day after day.

Being a school-gater is like being Royalty. You must watch what you do, dress soberly, walk in a straight line. And *never* drop cigarette ash into anyone's pram. It's for your own good. Very soon your child will become desperate with worry if he thinks you are not exactly like everyone else. So leave your fun fur and your monocle at

home, and be sure you are arrayed in easycare poly-cotton for the 3.30 inspection.

On his first day he'll be out on the dot, touchingly glad to be with you and unbuttoned everywhere. His shoes will be on the wrong feet, his shirt tail will be flying free and he will smell of Mrs Robinson. He'll be full of news as well. Of the pictures he has drawn, of who was sick and who called Mrs Robinson fat, and how he has to have his name on his painting apron by tomorrow *without fail*. It has started. With minor variations you are going to go through this thousands of times. The tyranny of what Mrs Robinson says.

Towards the end of his first week he will start to bring things home with him. Other people's PE shorts, letters about Harvest Festival, grazed knees, and small ruthless-looking boys called Wayne. He'll say, 'Wayne wants to play with me.' You'll say, 'Perhaps another day when I've had a chance to arrange it with Wayne's Mummy.' Wayne will say, 'My Mum don't mind. I'll come today.' And, when you ask him where his Mummy is, he'll tell you she's gone home and he's got to be back by eight. He won't know where he lives and no one else will admit to even recognising him. You might as well try to give a stray dog the slip. He'll follow you home, tolerate your funny eating habits and then expect you to drive three circuits of the town trying to find a front door that looks familiar. If you ever find her, his mother will take delivery of him without a word and she will look at you as though you are quite mad. The next afternoon it won't be Wayne. It will be someone else.

Sometimes it will happen the other way round. Sometimes it will be Geoffrey who's stowed away in the back of someone else's motor. While he's very young you can deal peremptorily with this sort of casual socialising. Just apologise pleasantly to the driver of the car and carry your child bodily from the scene. If he screams, scream back. If he holds his breath and goes stiff, carry him like a paperhanger's table. Soon he'll reach the age where he will die rather than have you make an exhibition of yourself, and then he will have the decency to make proper arrangements, written into diaries and ratified by all the adults concerned.

After a week or two, Mrs Robinson will move into your life in a big way. Her opinions on everything, from the nicest colour for a dressing gown to the long-term prospects for a drop in interest rates, will be relayed to you every afternoon in a torrent. She will think something definite about everything and her confidence in the correctness of her views will be so infectious that, before long, your Geoffrey will be willing to swear that black is white, on the strength that Mrs Robinson said so.

You'll be prepared to go to quite a lot of trouble not to upset Mrs R. Naturally you'll want to smooth the path your child must tread in any way you can, and sucking up to his teacher is an obvious step for you to think of taking.

Don't bother. You'll be wasting your time. Mrs Robinson has been looking for the perfect parent for years, and she just knows she's never going to find it. It's because she has trouble with proportion. If you spent all day in a room full of very small chairs, you'd probably end up the same way. If thirty little herberts kept reminding you how big and wise you were, come Home Time that playground would look to you as it does to her. Full of oversized tearaways with Sainsbury's carrier bags. We hear a lot about the pressures on this underpaid profession, but not a word about how long it takes at the end of the day for their perception of size and importance to return to normal.

In Mrs Robinson's book, the worst thing you can be, apart from a mass murderer, is a Working Mother. By Working Mothers I don't mean the millions who spend their days running a house, raising children and watching *Pebble Mill at One*. Work they certainly do, and mothers they certainly are, but, as long as they mop up, fill the cake tins and keep stumm, who could say a cross word against them? I'm talking about women who turn their backs on their children and hold their hands out for wages. Low, contemptible creatures grasping at grubby pound notes. Twilight people. They do not make a pretty sight. I know because sometimes I look in the mirror.

Most weeks you can find an article on working mothers in some magazine. It will be about someone with a Filipino in the loft and a wardrobe full of tailored wool. She'll have planned her career very astutely, have a perfectly wonderful partner who works freelance from home, and isn't *that* jolly handy, and she manages her time and her Filofax so ruthlessly that she's always home for at least one bath night a month.

Then there's the rest of us. We don't earn enough to give a Filipino or any other human being a living wage, we can't take our work home and catch up while we rock the fevered cradle, and we do work of such head-banging futility that, when we get home, all we want to do is scratch where our pantyhose has been pinching, and go to sleep. We do it for money. But as far as Mrs Robinson is concerned we do it to make ourselves unavailable.

How can your children possibly feel free to catch mumps or stay late at school for Chess Club if you are gadding around snagging your tights in Retail Administration and giving to farewell collections for people who have managed to tunnel out? What if Mrs Robinson says she'll have to have a word with you, *immediately*? What if Geoffrey's shoe laces break?

You won't be there, that's what. Ever. You can organise your annual leave so that you don't miss Speech Day, but you will never be there for the impromptu highs and lows, because there will be something every single day. You may have stayed up till midnight finishing the hem on Robin Hood's Lincoln Green, and done a turbo-charged shop in your lunch hour for a Dangermouse pencil sharpener and grey socks to fit a small but growing lad, but, when that phone rings with the news that Hammy the Hamster is no more and Mrs Robinson says *everyone* should have a cooked breakfast, your support hose will not be strong enough to take the strain of knowing that back in the old home town, Mrs Robinson is laying all of society's ills at your very door.

You'd be surprised how much undressing goes on in schools today. They do the same in cloakrooms as they ever did – hanging their coats on their pegs and then sky-diving out of them, but they do a lot more besides. They change their shoes every time the caretaker breathes. They change into T-shirt and shorts for half an hour of

Being A Tree to Mrs Robinson's Dansette. And most days, in the lunch hour there is a game of strip poker. I know this because one day your child will come home in someone else's vest.

Basically he will come home wrecked, but there will be seasonal variations to watch for. If it's November, he will be half naked; if it is a wet November, he will be wearing two left Wellingtons; and, if it is July and it's turned out fine, Mrs Robinson will have force-fed him into his duffle coat, Swedish ski-hat and windproof leggings and sent him out across the blistered tarmac to beg for mercy and a cold drink. Later on, when this freakish July weather has given way to the sort you would have expected, Mrs Robinson will keep them all in late. About ten minutes late. She'll have a perfect view of you, drowning, not waving. She'll be able to see all those animals queueing up in pairs to get aboard the school coach. But she'll carry on handing out those letters about Parents' Evening, and she'll do it *real slow*.

When you get that letter home and dry it out, you'll find there is a little tear-off slip to send back, saying whether you'll be going or not. You will be going. It looks very bad if you don't. Even if you are sure there'll be nothing to talk about, accept the invitation. You never know. And, once the date is in your diary, let nothing stand in your way. You may have to turn down more tantalising offers, bolt your food and pay good money for a babysitter. Never mind. Just get your can down there. I once travelled seventy miles and appeared dressed in black tie and plastic diamonds, and I was glad I had, I can tell you. I was there for the launch of my daughter's Busy Book. And that made it a night to remember.

Geoffrey's work will be there for you to look at. Heaps of it. Smudgy pages of Fletcher Maths, and all a lad needs to know about dinosaurs, with the words sliding down a very steep gradient. And then his Busy Book.

I don't know that they should let us read them. I accept that children should write about what's going on in their lives, and that their teachers must read what they've written. I don't even mind them having a quiet snigger. It must be one of the few perks they get, apart from indecently long holidays and hundreds of small people thinking that they're God. But shouldn't we parents be spared entries like 'On Sunday we had chips we always have chips and Mummy got the big nife that Nanny says is dangerous in a house with children and she said if Daddy didn't shut up she'd stik it in him but she didn't and then we had an icecream'? I *mean*, we all know how children exaggerate. We don't *always* have chips. But no matter how praiseworthy a life you lead, even if you're a blood donor *and* collect for Christian Aid, you will come off that page reading like a cross between Ivan the Terrible and Pig Pen. How can you hold your head up and enquire about the quality of Geoffrey's number work, when Mrs Robinson knows he comes from a malnourished family of uncommon violence, and you know she knows?

You may have to wait around until it's your turn for frank disclosure, but there will be interesting things to look at. The Nature Table, for instance. Or the terrible state of the school brickwork. And other parents. Not shy and reticent like they are at the school gate, but paired and confident. Some will not have their jacket fastened by a safety pin. These are the parents of children who do not have penicillin growing inside their lunchboxes. Children whose Busy Books are full of ripping yarns about games of Cluedo in the bosom of the family. But don't worry. There will be some of the other sort as well. Fidgeting in case they're not home in time for *A Question of Sport*, checking their fly, and daring their other half to even think of opening their mouth and letting the whole family down. You'll see all these people again and again, and, on less harrowing occasions, like Sports Day and the Christmas Concert, they may even speak to you.

Christmas concerts can be a joy, provided you have not had to spend the preceding month living with the Blessed Virgin or the Archangel Gabriel. If you have, pity help you. Far better to be the parent of a Lowing Ox, or at most The Innkeeper. They may not get such lavish notices, but there's a lot less melodrama if they forget their lines. Furthermore, stars who have had rave reviews tend to come over all unnecessary when it's time to wipe off the greasepaint and drink up their Horlicks.

Get to the Christmas concert early. All the best seats will be reserved for the school governors and others of noble birth, so you will have to jostle for the second-best ones. You can pass the time until the curtain goes up mugging up on the words to Hark the Herald, and observing Hurricane Hilda.

Every Christmas concert needs helpers. Kind people to make shepherd's crooks and deal with fainting camels. But there will only be one Hilda. If you're stricken with flu and miss her this time, you'll get other chances. At the Easter Fayre, the Summer Fête, and up to her elbows in marrows at Harvest Festival.

This woman will be a real mover. She'll have a body like a Chieftain tank, a face that speaks of contented indispensability, and a very tired-looking husband propped up on a well-placed seat. She will have made all the costumes, baked four hundred meltingly light mince pies and been back at the school in time to strap the heavenly host into their wings and ensure that Joseph does not go AWOL. She is walking proof that you can be in more than one place at the same time. She will be Assistant Stage Manager, Head of Catering, and Co-ordinator of Shepherd's Headdresses and Dry Knickers, running around with a mouth full of kirbygrips and slipping out with needless ostentation just before the interval, because two hundred glasses of weak orange squash are needed in the Green Room. It's probably something to do with her thyroid.

As an ordinary mortal, all that will be asked of you will be the odd length of dressing-gown cord and lots of generous applause. No problem. At some point in the evening I guarantee something will move you to tears. Apart from Hurricane Hilda.

You'll generally get two tries at Sports Day, on account of the first one getting rained off. Second time round, you'll need an air ring for your pressure points, a large well-chilled bottle of lemon barley water *or something* and an informed interest in novelty races. You should also wear a good bra or have your leg put in a plaster cast for the afternoon. I'll tell you why in a minute.

Hilda will be there with her sleeves rolled up. While she is holding the finishing tape and making sure you all get to the end of the race card on time, you should be paying close attention to what's happening on track. Children's races are over very quickly and, if you're busy rubbernecking at someone who has turned up with Bermuda Shorts and an Unknown Man, you will miss what you are supposed to be watching – young Geoffrey getting headed at the last hurdle from home in the Boys' Steeplechase.

Sports Day is the day when the ones who can't read have the last laugh. The ones who shine least in the classroom are often the ones who can shift fastest when they're let out onto grass. By the time the swots come shambling in with their library books under their arms, the winner will have had a shower, a shampoo and a sherbet dab and the Hurricane will have the next bunch under starter's orders.

Right at the end of the afternoon, when it starts to look like rain and you're wondering whether they'll scrub the Country Dancing display, the moment will arrive when you see the point of pretending to be on crutches. There'll be a Mothers' Race. There will also be a Toddlers' Race, and, if your school isn't in an area where fathers are an endangered species, there will also be a Fathers' Race.

Toddlers' Races always have an enormous field. About two of them will be raring to run the course, and the other fifty will be crying to go home. If you have an eligible toddler and you must put her through this ordeal, your best plan is to get yourself down to the finish with a balloon and a tin of Quality Street and make sure she can see you. This is the only certain way of getting her to move an inch.

Fathers' Races can get very heavy. And I'm not just talking vibrations. There will be a lot of muttering down on the rail about how have all these men managed to get the afternoon off. Despite role reversal, flexi-time and a world recession, a man with time to stand in a sack and jump still excites comment. Also, fathers like to win. Where a mother would settle gratefully for not falling over, a father will want to prove that he's still in pretty good shape. There'll be a lot of elbowing and horseplay and a closely fought finish, with the race won by no more than a belly. Of course it's the taking part that counts. So they say.

If you are not in plaster or at least significantly bandaged, the Mothers' Race will be unavoidable. Hilda will be operating a three-line whip. Now do you understand about wearing a good bra? No sense in waiting until you've had to carry them one hundred yards, one in each hand, before an audience of thousands, and then thinking about it. Batten them down, kick off your shoes, check you're pointing in the same direction as everyone else and then *run*. Sometimes, putting a drop of something in the lemon barley water helps.

Now there is more to school than Egg and Spoon races and biblical tableaux. There is work to be done. Unless you are very rich or very young, don't expect your children's school to be anything like your own. Times have changed. Classrooms are airy, cheerful places. There are televisions and radios and computers, and hardly anything is taught by monotonous repetition. If you particularly want your child shackled to a desk carved with the initials of boys who died at Passchendaele, you will have to pay for it. Learning by rote, corporal punishment and dead languages are all still there for the having, as long as you have enough cash. Otherwise, your child is going to spend the next eleven years enjoying himself as he tries to remember how many beans make five. You may feel a little edgy about the other lot, conjugating themselves silly over in the spartan, private sector. Aren't they learning a lot more over there, free from the distractions of laissez-faire? Yes, they are. Aren't they going to mop up all the university places, swamp the professions and generally nobble all that is brightest and best? Funnily enough, not necessarily. If Geoffrey does his homework he may still come out of it all quite nicely.

Homework creeps up on you. It starts off as a few pages of a reading book that have to be listened to, or a simple project like making a telephone out of a piece of string and two empty cocoa tins. Just tell me who ever has two empty cocoa tins at the same time? At this stage, homework is more a test of what useful things you've got hidden in your cupboards than it is of your child's intellect. To start with, you won't go far wrong if you are never without tracing paper, a ruler, and a packet of chocolate digestives. In a few years time, you will also need a pot of strong coffee, your wits and a shelf of reference books. I would never bother with encyclopaedias. They can come in handy for flattening out rolls of carpet, but that's about all. Far better to have a bird book and an astronomy book and a book that tells you how many yards of tubing you've got inside you. Then you'll need a dictionary, an atlas that's cheap enough to dump when all the African countries have changed their names again, and another packet of biscuits. The idea is that you dunk them in your coffee and make encouraging noises, while Geoffrey looks up the answers. You should only empty your mouth and wade in when you absolutely have to. If you pop up, all bright-eyed, the moment he starts chewing the end of his pencil, he'll lose confidence in his ability to do any of it on his own. He may need no more than a nudge in the right direction, or a square or two of Fruit & Nut when he starts to run out of steam. Or his problem may be that he doesn't really know how to look things up. If that's the case, give him a telephone directory and a train timetable and let him practise.

If he does get absolutely stuck, keep your help simple. You may well have A-level Maths but, if Geoffrey's trouble is that his circles go wonky when he tries to use a pair of compasses, this is not the moment for you to show off. It *is* hard to keep your hands in your pockets when his ten lines on the Norman Conquest look like a drink-crazed flea has been at the ink and you desperately want a gold star, but you must. I won a prize once for my collection of wild flowers. They presented me with a book about trees. I've still got it somewhere, but it should have been my mother's name they wrote inside the front cover. She was the one who dragged me half way round Leicestershire searching for specimens in all weathers. She got me the right book out of the library and bought the blotting paper for pressing the flowers under a pile of encyclopaedias. (I knew I'd think of something else you can use them for.) She helped me stick them in, told me what to write and conspired with me to defraud the Education Authority of a prize to the value of five shillings. To this day all I know about wild flowers is that buttercups look lovely in a jam jar, and they all look a lot nicer than chrysanthemums.

As the years pass and you eat more biscuits of an evening, you will progress from being a school-gater. The need for you to arrive punctually, smile warmly and carry home a portfolio of damp

paintings will dwindle. He'll get old enough to manage the journey on his own, and, provided you scream at him about not going off with nice strangers, and, provided you still turn up on the days he has to carry his double bass home, that will be the best arrangement. He won't mind letting himself in if you are delayed by the day's business. In fact he'll really *like* letting himself in. He'll be able to drink a litre of apple juice, be sick without you being there to say I told you so, *and* be able to watch all of *Grange Hill* without taking his coat off. This is when being a Working Mother starts to have its advantages.

If you must meet him from school, it is vitally important that you do not force upon him kisses or piggy-back rides. Remember this particularly once his voice has broken. The best thing will be to pretend you are nothing to do with him. It will help you to make the transition to your next role as the parent of a school-age child: the transition to Signer of Cheques. These will be for educational cruises to Tel Aviv, broken windows, trousers to replace the ones you bought last week to replace the ones you bought the week before that, and food. At school he will now be leading a life quite separate from you. His conversations will be full of people you've never met, he will be able to deal with little difficulties like a lost jockstrap all on his own, and his teachers, who are an altogether sounder lot on account of being able to look their kids in the eye and not having their classrooms full of dolls' house furniture, will be wise enough to know that Geoffrey is his own man. This is good. It takes a lot of pressure off you.

It's just a pity he still comes home smelling of Mrs Robinson.

I wouldn't be a kid for anything these days. From the moment someone fixes a Goosey Gander mobile above her cradle until the day she collects her Duke of Edinburgh Gold Medal, she never gets a minute to herself. She's forever climbing in and out of a car on her way to some extra-curricular activity, with a hyperactive woman at the wheel. It worries me. When does today's child ever get a quiet moment to kick a ball monotonously against an outside wall, or pick the scab on her knee?

The second car is to blame for a lot of it. I had devoted parents but I never got to have accordion lessons because it would have meant such a long wait for a bus. Now you can stand outside any school gate and watch the cars move off laden with little gymnasts and swimmers. A lot of them look like they'd be happier going straight home for a Penguin and a cuddle with the cat. But they can't because they have demented, upwardly mobile mothers intent that their family shall leave no experience untested. They fix up all the classes they can, and, if they're left with a spare evening, it haunts them until they find something to fill it. An Improvers' Class for Stamp Collectors. *Anything*. The whole affair has reached epidemic proportions and it's easy to see why. What sort of parent is going to sit idly by and let its child fall behind in the scramble to attain a smattering of everything? If everyone else's child is going for their bronze at swimming and your child still cries at the smell of chlorine, it can be a very worrying time.

But hold on. As a woman for whom the microwave oven and the second car have not yet happened, and for whom time and money are always in short supply, let me tell the rest of you who live on credit and travel on foot something important. Our children will be fine. The benefits of all that frantic leisure activity are illusory. All that happens is that a lot of children try and give up on a lot more things than ever they used to.

My recommendation is for no more than one activity for each child. More than that and the child will get exhausted, you will get exhausted, and worse, she will never have the time she needs for doing absolutely nothing. Watching television doesn't count. Just because it takes up a lot of time and you can't remember any of it five minutes after it has finished, doesn't make it the same as doing nothing. But it is very popular, so we should talk about it. Ever had that feeling that in about five hundred words' time you're going to be thoroughly ashamed of yourself?

The only easy way out of television is to put it back in its cardboard box and have it taken away. Or, if you are very strong, you could keep it in its box until someone is laid up with chicken pox and needs her mind taking off how much she itches and how crumpled the sheet keeps getting. Of course, if I only had myself to consider I would get rid of it tomorrow. I only ever use it for the news and weather. Maybe a bit of racing. *Afternoon Plus* if ever I'm home in the daytime. Apart from that, I only ever watch really good plays and documentaries and the ski-ing if I'm not working on a Sunday. As far as I'm concerned it could go and I'd never miss it. But children can get such a lot of pleasure from it, provided what they watch is carefully limited and monitored. All right, all right! For Chrissakes, I'm an ordinary woman! I get tired. I have things on my mind. Even though I know they're seeing far too much Zap and Pow, I don't often have enough spirit to say the television is staying off *all* evening *and* follow it through when I'm faced with cold turkey in the form of four pairs of socked feet being rubbed mindlessly up and down the wallpaper, and a great whimpering of Nothing to Do. And, now they're getting older and staying up later, what am I to do when I've been using my brain all day and want to collapse for an hour in front of *Cagney and Lacey*? Blindfold them?

You *can* learn a lot from television, if you choose your programmes carefully. But your children won't. They will gravitate naturally towards *Masters of the Universe* and *Duty Free*, and carrying on like that never got anyone into Imperial College.

The answer to television lies in how much time and energy you are prepared to put into controlling it and whether your budget can stretch to a video recorder. If it can't, you have the choice of chiselling their viewing hours into tablets of stone, being there at all times to enforce these and not being daunted by the names they will call you, *or* you can stop wishing they weren't watching the same trash as everyone else's children and be prepared occasionally to stoop to the unplumbed depths of *Crossroads* and *Knight Rider*, so that, when you carp, you really know what you're carping about.

If a video recorder is within your means, it all becomes a lot easier. You'll need a *Radio Times*, either flat so you can read the programme times or rolled up to strike anyone who touches any of the buttons, and you'll then be able to record what you are willing to let them see and tell them when they are allowed to look at it. No more channel-changing blood baths, no more bolted meals, and no more late nights you all regret the next morning.

Television apart, there are plenty of honourable pursuits for children which do not involve a twenty-mile round trip. Like playing cards.

Cards are good, provided things don't get nasty. Never bet, not even for Dolly Mixtures – particularly not for Dolly Mixtures – and stick to the simpler games like Pontoon, or, if you have a fortnight to spare, the game we call Strip Jack Naked and you probably call That Bloody Game That Goes On Forever. Talking of which, there's always Monopoly. This is now available in French as well as English so you can appeal to the baser side of human nature and learn which sections of the Parisian property market are ripe for speculation. Then there are chess and draughts and dominoes, and good old marbles. Marbles have recently made a big comeback and I for one am pleased to see it. They are cheap.

You play stretched out on the floor so they are excellent if you're feeling at all tired and emotional. *And* they may satisfy that strange urge we all get, to collect things. Long live marbles!

And darts. Provided they are out of doors. Darts are wonderful for the hand, the eye and the brain, but not so good for what estate agents call excellent decorative order. That's why our darts board hangs on a fence and our children wonder how it is that Jocky Wilson manages to play without woolly gloves. Every family should have a bag of marbles and a darts board. As well as a couple of skipping ropes, a card of extra strong knicker elastic and a bucket full of mildewed tennis balls. The skipping ropes are obvious. They are for playing at horses, and lashing the smallest child in the family into a doll's pushchair. The knicker elastic is for French Skipping. This is a very exhausting activity that gets them very nimble on their feet and reluctant to come in for their tea. And the tennis balls are for hitting into other people's gardens.

As you can see, I'm a great believer in fresh air for children. Fresh air and the minimum of equipment. They can do such a lot with nothing more than their own bodies. Leapfrogging, running up and down the street, hiding from each other, and leaning on lamp posts pitying people who listen to Dire Straits. This can fill up weeks of their lives without their ever setting foot in the house. Your only contact with them will be messages shouted through the letter box, like 'A bee stinged me two times and can we have ten boxes of Sun-Pat raisins?' and 'When is teatime?' If the snow starts to drift and you feel you cannot decently ask them to stay out any longer, life immediately becomes more complicated.

Out in the street or the garden an adult is the last person children want to see. Cricket can last all week provided adults with T-shirts and beer bellies don't muscle in. A forty year old in flip-flops who once fancied himself as a spin bowler, even though no one else did, is death to the summer game. But indoors the opposite is true. Indoors everything a child thinks of doing needs an adult on call, for translating Japanese instructions or dashing out to the shops at 5.25 for tubes of glue. A housebound child will wait until ten minutes

NOW!

before a meal is due to be served and then want to start on a crinoline bridal gown for Crystal Barbie. Or she will have seen something made on *Blue Peter* and want to make a start on it *immediately*, albeit that the frozen peas are coming to the boil and you are clean out of stiff card and dowelling.

These sort of activities are fine, when you can give one child your undivided attention. But it's no good, when you have to accommodate HMS *Victory* in three hundred pieces, a pictorial tribute to Madonna that is still in production, a knitter of the knit-one-drop-one persuasion *and*, out in the kitchen, things are hotting up. At times like this, simple, independent activities are called for. Like drawing pictures. Or picking your toenails with your mind completely out of gear. *Or doing your frigging music practice*!

So here we are. We have arrived at the sort of activities each child should only do one of. Activities that require regular practice, if there is ever to be any sense of progress and achievement. Like learning to play a musical instrument.

With music there are no half measures. Either you do it properly or not at all, and, if it is to be done properly, you will need a lot of dedication to sustain you on your way.

Music starts very simply with children. You sing them a few nursery rhymes and that's about it, until they are old enough for the descant recorder.

You may have heard the sound a recorder makes. We all have our shortcomings so let me say generously that the recorder is light, cheap and simple to master at the most basic of levels. A child can learn how to get a few notes out of a recorder quite quickly, so it can make a rewarding start for her, and it is not an impossible instrument to live with. I co-habit with three recorders, a tone-deaf singer and a person who whistles through his teeth, and the men in white coats haven't called to collect me yet. But, with any musical instrument, some learn faster than others. Knowing how to get a tune out of a recorder yourself can come in very handy when Abigail starts to flounder at school. This is when she'll want to jack it all in and audition for the shinty team instead. But she has started, so she should finish, and learn once and for all that one swallow doesn't make a summer, and one sprint through Pollywollydoodle doesn't make a James Galway.

A recorder is a good test of her true intentions when it comes to piano lessons and all the rest. Some parents go ahead with music lessons regardless, and I wish I had a fiver for every adult I know who started to learn and wishes they'd carried on. They didn't carry on because their mother got tired of yelling, 'Get down off that coal bunker and give your oboe some attention!'

I suppose nothing will imbue a child with a deep love of music quite the same way as a deranged mother who has just paid good money for a new cello string. But there we are. The child must learn that even modest control of an instrument takes time and trouble. And, if you are willing to rip the back seat out of your motor to make room for her harp, the very least she can do is practice playing it.

If she does practice, you will eventually get involved in Music Festivals. They go on all day. On and on. While ordinary people are running amok with their Marks & Spencer Charge Card, you will be stuck in a dusty hall listening to clarinet solos and rooting for your own flesh and blood. She won't win. She'll be robbed of first place by someone whose mother is wearing hand-knitted stockings and knows when to clap. She and her Mum will be regulars at these occasions, and they'll know everyone else who's there. They're an incestuous lot at Music Festivals.

But, if she never gets that far, a few months toying with that descant recorder will not go to waste. It will enjoy a new lease of life as a two-note police siren or an instrument of torture for wet Sunday afternoons, and in twenty-five years' time she may still remember enough of the basic fingering to help one of her own children get through 'O Come All Ye Faithful'.

With dancing classes you meet a different crowd. Instead of obscure jokes about inverted sevenths, and name-dropping about remote acquaintance with John Amis, you get straightforward bitching. It's always about the way certain children are turned out, and, the more disciplined the dance form, the fussier everyone gets about the gear. Propped up against the barre I have heard some pretty arch remarks about the grubbiness of certain knickers and the evident unironedness of certain shoe ribbons. I write as a woman for whom biological washing powders came too late, a woman whose washing has always been subject to everyday greyness of notable intensity. In a dancing school everything must be just right. The length of the tunic, the shade of the wrap-around cardigan, and the spring freshness of the underwear that occasionally bobs into view. And, if your child sticks at it long enough to get into the chorus line of the annual show, you will find yourself with a full-time job as chauffeur, hair crimper, and stitcher of several miles of fairy-dell tutu netting.

It all gets quite feverish, especially if your child is the only boy in the class. Boys are such rarities in smalltime ballet schools that they scarcely get a minute off stage at show time.

They are better represented in other dance forms, though. These days there are plenty of them doing modern dance and tap dancing, where they can have fun without all that pickiness over what everyone is wearing and whether they can curtsey nicely to Madame at the end of the class. Curtseying's not all that important. It might come in handy for the one in a million who gets to the Royal Ballet School, or if the Queen Mother drops in to see how things are rubbing along. But, if the bus service is anything like it was, I doubt she'll bother.

The only thing I'll say against tap dancing is that it's as compulsive as the eating of dry-roasted peanuts. You'll find she tap dances *everywhere*. Your parquet floors will never be the same again. Apart from that, I'd recommend it. Provided she isn't already signed up for Pony Club and Junior Gymnastics. Remember, we all need time for mindlessness.

Junior Gymnastics is a modern disease. I lay a lot of it at the door of poor little Olga Korbut. Someone put the word about that, if we were ever to beat those damned Slavs, we would have to start our children as young as they do and keep them toddling along that beam no matter how much they may beg to go to Boys' Brigade instead. Happily the British tradition of pussy-footed half-heartedness prevailed. As a nation we are incapable of being so cruel to the young. If you have a child who has a hankering for gymnastics, you can join her up without the least fear that she'll end up with doctored hormones and an Olympic Gold Medal. She'll become better co-ordinated, better balanced, and she'll learn how to fall. Then, when she has tired of Gym Club and she wants to play Junior League Football, if she also has a safe pair of hands you may have a little goalkeeper in the making.

Saturday football is basically cold. It is running up and down the side line screaming, 'Mark that boy!' and wishing you had got up in time to make a thermos of soup. It is also being certain it was someone else's turn to bring the orange quarters and the Mars Bars, it is a car full of other children griping because they don't qualify for Mars Bars and they are missing *Saturday Superstore*, and it is mud. But it does bring a flush to their cheeks, it demonstrates that a football pitch feels longer than it looks when you've run up and down it for half an hour, and it teaches them that you can't always win but, when you do, it feels bloody fantastic.

Ditto rugby, hockey, cricket, netball and anything else where they serve quartered oranges at half time – provided the parent whose turn it was to bring them has remembered.

I hesitate to mention horses alongside ordinary hobbies. It has to do with the horse. Children develop a strong sense of the horse being a living creature, in a way they never do for their football coach or their ballet Madame. A sense, quite rightly, that horses cannot be picked up and put down like knitting, because every minute of every day someone has to be seeing to their needs. For this reason I think horsiness is a trait best cultivated in the whole family, or strangled at birth. Any member of your family who wants to ride is going to end up wanting to do a lot more than just ride.

A stable yard is as fine an example of perpetual motion as you will ever see. Horses drink like Irishmen. They feed little and often. If they are stable-kept they also sweat and crap in their bedrooms, and, because of the life they lead, they need their feet attending to oftener than many a chap changes his nylon shirt.

Then there's all that leather wear. It needs sponging, and soaping and polishing, and generally leaving in a commendable state of cleanliness. Young Abigail is going to want to get involved in all of this. If she's really horsey, one of the first things she will have realised is that getting up on Cracker's back once a week and asking him to Walk On is no way to nurture their relationship. The best thing would be if the whole lot of you got yourselves down to the stables as often as possible and joined in, or if you gave horses a miss and just watched the show jumping on the telly. Left alone with her passion, Abigail will bore you all knickerless with talk of Kimblewick snaffles and how Cracker came to cast a shoe. How about swimming?

This is something everyone should learn, unless they have seen the *Poseidon Adventure* and decided they would prefer to die quickly. In my day, swimming lessons were something you had for health reasons. We asthmatics were taken by the coachload to inhale the fumes at the gas works and, if we didn't respond to that, we were made to tremble in the Corporation Baths, where boys with Brylcreemed hair passed water. You can tell how long ago that was: Brylcreem was still the thing. The idea was to frighten the asthma out of us, but it didn't work on me. To this day, if I catch sight of a rolled towel or a coin-in-the-slot hair dryer, I have to get out my inhaler.

But things have changed a lot. So much so that you see newborn babies turning up for swimming lessons. Our local pool has palm trees, and uni-sex changing rooms, and, instead of being shaped in a harsh rectangle, with a pile of shrouds folded neatly by the deep end, this place is shaped like a clover leaf, and it is impossible to guess whether you are about to drown or strike your knee on the bottom. I just wish someone could tell me why the science that brought the palm tree to Bletchley still cannot come up with a worthwhile drinks machine? And why thirty years on there are still boys piddling in the water and getting away with it?

But, as I was saying, they start them young at swimming these days. They bring her along, desperately keen not to waste any time. After kicking up a stink until they got a Leboyer birth, they are determined to have her swimming like a fish before she can sit up. So they strip her off at the poolside and slide her into the water in their arms. When her little body freezes into alarmed rejection they keep jumping her up and down in all that chlorinated urine and shouting 'Weeeeeeeee!' Do you know what really bothers me about these babies in the pool? Right! I mean, I know disposable nappies are marvellous these days, but they must have their limits.

You *can* teach a baby to swim. I know a family that had most of its children back in the days when you gave them all inflatable air rings and screamed, 'Fall into that bloody water and I'll kill you!' Then they had a late arrival, much adored and destined for early swimming. At the age of five she could outswim me and still have enough energy to open a packet of crisps, but her parents became terminally boring and none of us invited them to dinner any more.

What you should do is wait until your child has reached the age of perfect bladder control and then ask someone else to teach her. Parents make terrible teachers. They push too hard, they ignore the pleadings of a nervous and untrusting learner, and they can never believe that they have spawned a child of such incredible dumbness.

There's always the Brownies. And the Wolf Cubs and the Woodcraft Folk and all that gang. Uniforms, vows and rules, all made as wholesome as uniforms and vows can ever be. And singsongs. Then there are the attainment badges: something a child can work for with a little help and encouragement from home. How well I recall the Year of a Thousand Rock Cakes. And the taxing business of Weaving a Useful Article. But I never saw shoes polished as well as they were done for Remembrance Sunday or such pride in standing to attention in a biting November wind.

Some people just like uniforms. If your child is one of them, why not make sure he learns something handy while he's earning the right to wear all that brass? Something like the Red Cross cadets. First aid is more useful than semaphore, and in the summer he'll get to put it into practice at every garden fête for miles around. If that doesn't appeal to him but he wants to join up, there are still all the military cadet corps, for drilling, brass bands and preparing to hold back the Communist hordes.

For the child who prefers to turn the other cheek there's Sunday school. Even in my day they tried to liven it up with lick'n'stick pictures of Best Loved Bible Stories and an outing to Mablethorpe every June, so I expect in these days of falling congregations and general godlessness the whole thing will have been made into perfectly wizard fun. The only thing is, it will probably curtail the

Sunday lie-in. If you normally have time to eat a three-course breakfast and catch the 8.42, this will not be much of a sacrifice to make. But, if like me, you spend your working life trying to get on and off of the M1, you may resent having to set the alarm clock on Sundays because Jesus wants Keith for a sunbeam.

If this is the case, stamp collecting might be an agreeable compromise. In fact, collecting anything is not a bad idea as long as you have somewhere to keep it all, and as long as the original idea to collect novelty pencil sharpeners or toenail clippings comes from the child and not from you. If it was your idea, it is you who secretly wants to do the collecting, so you should come out of the closet and say so – even if what you want to collect is unwearable earrings of startling vulgarity. Then you can leave your child in peace to collect empty pop bottles, draw pictures of Dolly Parton in the condensation on his bedroom window, and generally enjoy his free time.

In a word, *DON'T*. Your children will provide you with all the mud and heartache you will ever need. But telling you that will not stop you. I'm still going to have to explain to you why you shouldn't have, why you just did, and what you can do about it now you've been silly.

You'll have heard people saying that a house is not a home without a bit of dog hair, and that pets are good for children. A lopsided opinion if ever I heard one. How do the pets feel about all this? Do they stay silent out of tact, or numb hopelessness? I need convincing that children and animals have anything to offer one another. And, if it's dog hair you're wanting, just send me a stamped addressed envelope.

It's a commonplace idea that, if a child grows up with animals, he will learn responsible attitudes towards the weak and defenceless, and get a bit of zoology thrown in. But it doesn't work. Responsibility for others is learned too slowly for the short-lived hamster to be of any help. It has to be practised on other human beings at regular intervals, in between practising responsibility for self. Some reach a creditable standard by the time they're middle-aged, but it's like reversing a car round a corner. Some people never get the hang of it. Zoology is something which is learned by careful, systematic observation and investigation. Walking past a hutch full of wet hay and miserable rabbit twice a day never taught anyone zoology.

The real reasons we keep pets are that we are prey to novelty, deaf to reason, and too ready to be seduced by anything soft and helpless.

Do something for me. Make a list of all the soft helplessness in your life. Are you sure you want more? I *do* understand the appeal of baby animals. You can pick them up and mess them around, and they don't talk back. But neither do animal-shaped nightdress cases or carpet slippers, and, at least when you tire of them, you can send them to a jumble sale and be rid of them for ever. Unless you too have the sort of children who queue all night outside jumble sales so they can buy back what you threw away.

But baby animals grow. They cost you, and inconvenience you, and get such a purchase on your heart strings that, when they fall sick and die, guilt and grief reduce you to a shadow. Think instead of giving a good home to a stray nylon bearskin rug, with head attached. It won't chew your milkman, you can run the Bex Bissell over it when it starts to smell rancid, and you'll never need to take it to the vet.

In spite of James Herriot, vets are still the sort of people I prefer to meet at drinks parties, if I have to meet them at all. No matter how baggily comfortable they look, I'd rather see the dentist any day. Somehow, all the happy, routine visits we have ever made for vaccinations and claw-clipping have faded away and I'm left with stark memories of a rabbit who was beyond help, and the dear, foul-breathed old dog who was there to take The Long Walk.

I'm willing to bet there's still a small part of you that believes a guinea pig is the very thing to get Albert through O-level Biology and help him relate in an affectionate way to his sisters. Am I right? Something small and furry? Something Albert can handle and feed and give a name to. Something that will smell.

If you choose a rabbit, the smell will stay outside, except on really hot days. With hamsters and mice and gerbils the smell will be about the same but it will seem worse because it will be in the confined space you call home.

The most exciting thing about any of them is combining the sexes in the right ratios so they can have babies. Finding a nest full of little pink squeakers is a surprisingly nice experience, even for nicotine-stained adults. So is following their progress over the first couple of weeks, and saying Requiem Mass for the ones that get squashed. After that it gets boring. For you and the hamsters. If you let them out to stretch their legs, they make a beeline for the inside of your

settee and won't come out until they've reduced its innards to
sawdust. If you let them have babies, the moment your advert
appears in the newsagent's window good friends will pretend not to
recognise you, and will hurry by on the other side, for fear of what
you might offer them. And no one *ever* wants to clean them out.
They talk about doing it, they hoard old newspapers for the
purposes of doing it, and they even draw up goddamned rotas, but
no one will ever get out there and DO IT.

If it's too late. If you have already fallen for one of these nibbling
stinkers, here is a crumb of comfort. They don't live long. Longer

than the average child's span of concerned interest, but nothing like as long as some of the other animals you shouldn't get. Like horses, and parrots, and tortoises.

If you are really into horses, you are probably well beyond friendly amateur help. Either you must ask your bank manager to deal with you very harshly, or you must muck out the bed you have made and lie in it.

A horse will eat your weekends and every five pound note you ever have. And, as if this is not enough, your table will keep disappearing under a load of something called Tack, and your children will pick up rude words and bad habits far above their station. The one thing I will say for a horse is that he won't hog the fire.

A parrot will also teach them new words and he won't cost you a packet in livery bills. What he will do is eat your wallpaper, excavate your plaster and outlive you. So you must make provision for him in your last will and testament.

And a tortoise is an unlovely thing that you must simply learn to do without. It is true they are part of Nature's rich variety, and that to other tortoises they are nothing short of essential, but there is no reason on earth for human beings to get involved with them. They don't do much except breathe, they have frail constitutions, and they are full of germs. I *know* they have them on *Blue Peter*. They make birthday cakes for dogs on *Blue Peter*, for heaven's sake. Think of it this way. You may not have thought much of North Africa, but tortoises really like it there. How about a cat?

Cats have a lot to be said for them. They don't care for too much undignified human grovelling, they take themselves for walks, and they never shit in their own backyard. And getting one is no problem. Provided all you want is a basic two-tone model with a leg at each corner, folks are giving them away all over the place. Choose one who's stayed home with his mum after the rest of the litter has gone. Don't be put off by what you know this can do to humans. A cat can learn a lot from his mum. She will have been short-tempered and fussy, and she will have taken a lot less time to knock her children into shape than you will.

If you need a little added stress in your life you can complicate things by spending a lot of money on a delicate breed or allowing him to get bossy about his food.

Do you remember the days when there was no such thing as cat food, and we all made our own entertainments? The days when a cat had to make do with what was left from the table and whatever he had the wit to catch for himself. Cats can still live like that. Farm cats do. That's why farm cats are unobtrusive and smart. That's the sort of cat you want.

If you have a cat before your first child is born, watch out. An established cat can get to worrying about security of tenure. There's a thriving market in cat nets for stretching over cots and prams, and with good reason. A warm, sleeping baby makes a very comfortable cushion for a cat with things on his mind. Supervise him closely for the first few months. If he's psychologically sound, he'll soon get back to ignoring people. Later it will be the child that must be supervised. You should not assume that, because your cat is capable of making a quick getaway, this is what he will choose to do. There may come a wet afternoon when he has nothing much else to do, when he decides to stick around and scratch the little bruiser who keeps getting hold of his tail. If your child has claw marks on his face, and the cat is off down the road with a red spotted handkerchief tied to the end of a stick, you can bet your life it wasn't the cat that started it.

Regretfully this brings me to dogs. I'd been putting it off, but the time has come.

Dogs start off as puppies. They have big eyes, waggy tails and at least four bendy legs. Please don't buy one.

A puppy is a full-time job. If you have children, that is another. Then, if you're going to market your own computer software, make all your own loose covers and complete an Open University Foundation Course, that's three more. And if you're expecting your first baby, shouldn't you be out somewhere learning how to bath a rubber dolly?

A puppy is a plague of locusts cunningly disguised so that you will love it at first sight. As soon as you get it home, you will see it for what it is – a demolition squad in a fur coat.

Here are some things a puppy will not eat. The Empire State Building. A high voltage steel pylon. And himself. Unless it's simply ages since he ate. Otherwise the world is, as you might say, his bowl of Butch. No need to cook it, sauce it or cut it up. Just leave it in a place you never thought he'd reach and he'll do the rest himself.

Here is another list. These are things actually eaten by an intelligent puppy who was getting ox liver, tripe, calcium-enriched puppy mixer and egg custard four times a day *and* a marrow bone that was just the right size to be dragged into her bed. Three pan scourers; a floor cloth; two *odd* sheepskin gloves; a Post Office First Day Cover; a silver napkin ring; three shrub roses. I am exaggerating slightly. She only changed the shape of the napkin ring, and, although she killed the roses, she wasn't such a pig that she ate them.

As you might expect of those who eat first and think later, puppies also do a lot of throwing up and squittering out. I can tell you that pan scourers pass straight through unchanged, sheepskin gives them diarrhoea and silver paper comes out as an interesting decorative finish – a sort of Fabergé dog turd. All of which is unhygienic, time-consuming and does not make for a good light-hearted read, but we're not through yet. Because, while he is eating everything that stands still, he will be picking up a few things that move: worms, ticks, fleas and anyone else that wants to come along for the ride. And, when you try to evict them, he won't give you an ounce of help. He'll pretend to swallow his worm pill and then look you steadily in the eye as he coughs it under the fence onto next door's patio. That's the trouble with dogs. They have no integrity.

When you're through with balancing his diet, mopping up his messes and purging him of squatters, it will be time to start training him. A puppy needs a lot of training. Without it he will grow into the average British dog. He will jump up, chase cars, bark endlessly and gradually occupy so much of your bed that you'll have to move out. Training should cure him of these vices, and you cannot start too soon. You must do it every day in short rewarding bursts, in between being a good parent, an upright citizen and a well-rounded human being with stacks of outside interests. See what I mean? And you must keep up this training lark until he is thoroughly Woodhoused.

Barbara Woodhouse is to puppies what Elizabeth David is to good food. Get one of Woodhouse's books and do as she tells you. One of the first things she will tell you is not to get a puppy if you have young children.

A fully-fledged dog is a different proposition from a puppy. Less bouncy, with the bad habits more deeply entrenched.

The nicest dogs are other people's, seen at a distance gambolling over Hampstead Heath. A dog of your own has needs, and unless you live in a large, shabby house set in large, shabby grounds with lots of large, shabby, open-air types who also love dogs, he will look to you for all his company and exercise. If your children are young, they won't be able to take him for walks or make him swallow his vitamin pill, and you'll be too tired. You cannot push a pram, lead the fulfilled life of a consenting adult, and exercise an Afghan hound. If your children are older, it will be no better. They will never think to walk him, feed him or worm him, they will complain bitterly when he sits on the Monopoly board and they will leave you to solve one of life's great and enduring mysteries. Where should a dog do what a dog has to do?

If you need a single, cogent argument to dissuade you from getting a dog, it has to be dog shit. The Western world is full of it. Some day the weight of it is going to shift the earth's tilt and we shall all find ourselves taking part in a disaster movie. Depend upon it.

If you are an idle slob and shove Fang out of the kitchen door every time he starts to circle purposefully, you will get no more than you deserve. Some morning you'll run barefoot across the grass to pluck a dew-fresh rose, and, the next thing you know, men in decontamination suits will be hosing you down. Fang will have turned your rolling lawns into a No Go area. And the word will have got round. 'Let's all go round to Fang's place, his people don't mind.' No more al fresco lunches. Nowhere to play footie. And absolutely no more early morning rose plucking. You can try shovelling it up before visitors are expected, but you'll miss one – the one the visiting child is going to stand on. Better really not to let your dog use your garden as a toilet. Ever. Better to take him out twice a day and get him to do it somewhere else. Like the footpath. Or someone else's garden.

Do you take my point? There is something about the normal bodily functions of a dog that make him disgusting to live with. He may be loyal, good-looking and second to none at fetching sticks, but, with a dog, the bottom line is always something nasty on the sole of your shoe.

Perhaps you were thinking of something more exotic? An aquarium, or a vivarium, or a jar of frog spawn? Wrong again. Not for your children at any rate. Really exotic things are for grown-up enthusiasts who aren't going to prefer ice hockey after three weeks and who aren't ever going to want to go to Disneyland or any other place you can't take a tank of fish. The odder the animal, the odder its diet is likely to be. What might you be letting yourself in for? Hatching your own flies? Slug hunts at first light? Is there anyone who will do it for you, if you fall down stairs and break both your legs? There isn't, is there? If you couldn't get anyone to give Albert his tea the day you got stuck at the Boat Show, because his nose never stops running and he won't eat eggs, who the hell are you going to get to drop a warm mouse in with the python?

Frog spawn is just plain inhumane. A marmalade jar of tap water is not the right habitat for two hundred tadpoles. Children can learn about the life cycle of the frog from a book, and, if schools insist on life studies, then I would have thought half a dozen tadpoles per school would be more than enough.

Animals in school are quite the thing these days. In my day, we were only allowed head lice and a boy called Victor, but times have changed. Before your child starts school, you should teach him how to wipe his bottom, how to deal with jerks who try to steal his Crunchy Bar, and how to sit on his hands when the teacher asks who would like to look after the hamster during the long summer holidays. This is because school hamsters usually wait until August to die. Then how are you going to feel? *If* you can find his dead ringer in a pet shop and get it home and caged before Reuters News Agency have wind of it, you may get away with it, but in August pet shops are full of desperate men clutching Polaroid shots of stiff school hamsters. You may not be one of the lucky ones. And, if you're not, come September you'll have to face five hundred pairs of accusing eyes *and* the dinner ladies.

The other contact you'll have with animals once you have children will be at the zoo. I can't explain why, but they never lose their appeal. A zoo is expensive to get into, expensive to run, and, despite all the money that changes hands at the turnstile, there's always a tatty, impoverished look everywhere you turn. What's worse, it doesn't take long for you to realise that, whatever else your children are getting out of the experience, it is certainly not a deeper understanding of the animal world. Our children did learn things at the zoo. They learned that there's never any toilet roll in the lavatories, that a tired grown-up will call nearly anything a Sort of Antelope, and that elephant poohs are just about the size you'd expect them to be. Anything else they know about animals they will have picked up from Johnnie Morris or our pile of dog-eared Ladybird books. Parked beside the flamingoes I have seen a child get very excited about a sparrow taking a dust bath. And, at the end of an arduous day of lions, tigers and big brown bears, I was interested to hear that what they had liked best was collecting the ring-pulls other people had dropped, and having chips in the car because Daddy was too pooped to cook.

The only sort of contact with animals that is remotely educational is business contact. Like on farms. Children who grow up on farms soon get the idea. Everyone is there for a purpose, no one gets fawned over, and it is plain for all to see who eats whom. We can't all be farmers, of course. But there are lots of people bringing up children in modest rural surroundings who like the idea of pretending. Keeping animals in a small way and hoping they might just about pay for their own board and lodging. Things like chickens and ducks. And the vile and dastardly goat.

Chickens and ducks are a marvellous way of introducing children to nature in the raw. You need a bit of space. You *can* play at farms in Hammersmith, but it will end in tears. None of your neighbours will speak to you, and one by one your animals will die terrible urban deaths. Chickens need somewhere dry to run, ducks need somewhere wet, and all of them need shutting away in a shed at night unless you are prepared to write rats and foxes into the script. There's nothing like a bit of poultry farming for illustrating what a hard old world we live in. If it's eggs you're after and there's more than two of you to feed, it's going to cost you money for extra chicken rations. If it's *Poule au Pot* or a crisply roasted duckling you're thinking of, you'd be better off going to Sainsbury's. Slices of meat that were once named Jemima can take the appetite clean away. But, if you want your children to learn about the tragedy of wanton vandalism, or that useful lesson in life about always watching your back, chickens and foxes make perfect examples. And, if you'd like your children to see just how lousy a mother can be, introduce them to a duck.

Fits of self-sufficiency take people in many different ways. I can only advise you that, if you have young children, you will do better with vegetables than with animals, and, best of all, with a couple of reclining chairs and a reliable local greengrocer.

If in a moment of pioneering folly, you find you have said Yes to a goat, there is only one thing to be done. Put it in a boat, row it out to an uninhabited island, and leave it there. Water is the only thing you can put round it that will keep it in. Before the Goat Lobby arrives to butt me into silence I must tell you that goats destroy gardens and friendships with versatile ease, that they are pathetically feeble about the British climate and that, if you want milk from them, they are very expensive to feed. You won't get owt for nowt from a goat. True enough, goat's milk is wonderful for children and invalids but, if you are trying to raise children or to get better, you shouldn't be trying to live with the most diabolical curry ingredient ever to stand on four legs. You can buy goat's milk in dandy little waxed cartons.

And a final word. Every family has someone in it who brings home birds with broken wings. Don't try to be Francis of Assisi. You do hear of savaged hedgehogs being brought back to life by warm milk and prayers, but generally they die. If I were a dying hedgehog, I guess I'd rather drag myself under a bush and do it My Way than spend my last hours in a shoe box being force-fed on Weetabix and asked to answer to the name Tiggywinkle. Wouldn't you?

If your idea of a holiday is poolside Camparis, dancing till dawn, and a seamless suntan, what you need is a vasectomy. Otherwise, I must tell you at once, we are talking buckets and spades.

The other thing I should tell you is that I don't really like holidays. I've been dragged away four times in the last sixteen years, never for more than a week, and I've been homesick every time, worrying about the rabbits being properly fed and developers moving our street somewhere we can't find it. If ever we get to afford to winter in Antigua I don't know what I shall do. Deface our passports probably.

Holidays are what we are all supposed to need from time to time. A change of view, a change of company, and an escape from work because most of us hate the way we earn a living. People who get paid for doing what they like best never feel tempted by boarding houses in Worthing, so they are doubly blessed. The rest of us are not so lucky. We need to go to Worthing from time to time to remind ourselves that work is not that bad after all.

When our children were very young, I always insisted that there was no need to travel as far as Sussex for me to have a change of lifestyle. Something much simpler would do for me. Like being locked in a soundproof booth for a night of unhampered sleep. Or just walking to the shops by a different route. Besides, it would have taken one of Pickford's biggest vans to get us to Worthing with all that gear.

The trouble is, once you have children, your view of holidays becomes blinkered. Two weeks with sea breezes, and it will have to be August because if you keep carting the boy off to Pontins in the middle of term he will never get his CSE Geography. Two weeks is a big mistake. If you're not rich and leisured enough to be able to take a house for the whole summer and fill it with friends, dying pot plants and all the things that turn a house into a home, you shouldn't settle for a fortnight. Ten days is as long as most of us can go, without missing what we've left behind. Longer than that and we start to feel anxious. The tension betrays itself in little ways. Hunched men walking into the wind by the edge of the ocean, dreaming of what they might do if only they were home with a toolbox handy. Women in Pakamacs buying novelty rock to ease the ache for their slippers and a decent cup of tea. People who have stayed too long. They should have gone home on Saturday and spent the second week trying to get rid of the sand.

On the scale of holidaying splendour, the pinnacle is reckoned to be staying in a hotel where everything is done for you, and rock bottom is reckoned to be a tent. This is the sort of inflammatory remark I would never make when face to face with a camper. Campers are very passionate people. They will defend their miserable practices with loud argument, line diagrams and grievous bodily enthusiasm. What could be better, they will say, than lying in a tent with the smell of your loved ones, listening to the rain and totting up how much money you're saving? Almost anything I'd guess. Offhand, I can only think of one thing worse. And that is lying in a tent knowing that just along the field there is an exorbitantly pricey supermarket selling all the dismal, second-rate food you have to put up with the rest of the year, and that, no matter what else you offer them, your children will prefer to spend the day playing Hide and Seek around the communal washhouse. I *know* camping is not what it used to be. I know there's no need to hang your billycan from a forked twig and forage for kindling. I know tents can have bedrooms and lounges and dinettes, not to mention dbl.gge., C H & ext.gdns.ld.t.lwn. I know you can run a telly off a power pack, keep things smart on a nifty open-air ironing board, and hardly notice you've left home. I still think it stinks.

Hotels can be awkward with small children. If you can afford one big enough to have Facilities with a big F, you may manage to get a few days of genuine rest. Invisible people will pick up your towels, shake out your duvet and help themselves to your perfume. Others will ply you with great trenchers of photographer's food. Lobsters, pineapples and whole sirloins of beef. You'll have to get on bended knee for a cheese sandwich, and all the influence in the world will not secure you a grapefruit *without* a glacé cherry.

This type of hotel may cater for children. If that's what it says in the brochure, then there are certain basic amenities you may rely on. You will be able to get a meal and a high chair at the unsocial hour of five o'clock without the maître d' having a seizure. There will be a purulent-looking paddling pool full of eighteen year old lads climbing on each other's shoulders. And there will be a Baby Listening Service. This is the real liberator. It will enable you to give the Sangria a real bashing and do silly dances to the Tweet Tweet Song, safe in the knowledge that twenty floors up – what if there's a fire, aaargh – if your little snugglebum so much as whimpers, there is a slim chance that the jaded creature painting her toenails in Reception will hear him and rush to let you know. Maybe.

At least in a small West Country guesthouse you won't have to worry about him waking. You'll be able to hear him from the dining room – you and all the other guests. Sometimes the people who run these establishments are so wonderful they will offer to babysit for you, properly, not twenty floors away with a dicky intercom. These saintly folk will also do packed lunches, smile every time your three year old slams their french windows, *and* offer you a choice of puddings. Some of them won't even make you go out on wet days. Not like the guesthouses of my childhood. There was one in Llandudno where dogs were welcome. It could be blowing Force Ten and they'd still lock you out and shout through the keyhole, 'Go up the Great Orme, there's lovely.' Unless you were a corgi. And one on the Isle of Wight where you *could* stay in, if it was very wet, because they didn't want you leaving wet coats all over the candlewick, but you had to keep your voices down, and the room where they kept The Pack of Cards was painted in Windsor Soup Brown after the style of Beryl Bainbridge.

If you have found a place where they remember your name and let you have your grapefruit without a cherry, you have found something precious. Your difficulty may be in *not* going back every year. You won't want to hurt their feelings. And there will be other regulars who want to pal up with you. People who are terrific fun in Bournemouth but you wouldn't be seen dead with in Wolverhampton, who send you Christmas cards marked, 'Here's to Moss Nook, first Saturday in August.'

There is an alternative. A compromise between flapping canvas and the airless dementia of a five-star hotel. Self-catering. With this, you just pay money to go somewhere else and do what you'd do if you'd stayed at home. Like all compromises it combines the worst of everything.

You can do it under a tiled roof or you can do it in a coffin-shaped sweatbox that is upholstered in a depressing shade of orange. This is also known as caravanning.

The first thing you should know about caravans is that children love them. The smaller the caravan, the better they like it, and once they've had sight of one they will pester you for more. The best way out of this difficult situation is to take them to a Caravan Show. It's a good, cheap day out. They'll race in and out of fifty different models finding the hidden cupboards, guessing how the gas hob converts into a fourposter bed, defecating in the For Display Purposes Only Elsan, and having an absolute whale of a time. With luck, this will get caravans out of their system and save you having a nervous breakdown in Paignton, when you could just as well be having one at home.

Imagine your own home with all the debris of normal activity and everyone being there at the same time. Add to it a collection of buckets, shrimping nets, cricket bats, flippers, 800-piece jigsaws, interesting seashells and shattered thermos flasks. Now reduce it all to the size of a wardrobe. This is what your caravan holiday will be like.

Caravans are fine for one or two adults, provided they are of a tidy disposition and can tolerate extremes of temperature. But, with young children, they are no more than a test of your ingenuity and your love for one another. If you must do it, embrace everybody warmly before you set out. Tell them you will not mean most of the things you'll be shouting at them. And tell them that the project is to see how little time you can spend awake and aware inside that wonder of planning economy.

If you self-cater inside bricks and mortar there will be a lot more room to spread, even if, when the brochure said sleeps six, it didn't mean all at the same time. As inflatable dinghies, decorative seaweed and broken flip-flops expand to fill the space available, you should set aside at least two days at the end of your holiday to return the house to the state in which you found it. Which, when you think about it, is a funny way to relax and refresh yourself for the year ahead. You have probably left behind fur-coated stairtreads and a sluggish U-bend, and they'll still be waiting for you when you get back. And here you are, within spitting distance of a trip round the bay and a clotted-cream tea, prowling with a damp J Cloth.

The very worst thing to do is to rent from friends. You'll feel you should emulsion right through and landscape the garden before you leave. And you won't even feel free to tell them what a pigging awful place you thought Broadstairs was.

The good thing about self-catering is that you can please yourselves. Even though you'll miss your old can-opener that only you has ever got the hang of, and all the warm jumpers you never thought you'd need, you will be as free as the birds. Get up when you like, eat when you like, and be under absolutely no pressure as long as you make sure there's enough milk before the shops close, think up something for tea that everyone will eat, keep the beach from reclaiming the house and play bat and ball with anyone who asks you.

This is no way to carry on. The only way to self-cater is to lay it on the line. Just a few house rules. No one has to cook who doesn't wish to. Whosoever has lain in a bed can get right back upstairs and make it. And, when a parent says he does not want to be buried up to his neck with his new Tom Sharpe, he means it. Equip each child with a box of his favourite breakfast cereal. Show him how regular use of a dustpan and brush can improve the sand situation. And tell them all every four hours what a marvellous time they're having.

So we have narrowed the sensible choices a little. To a friendly family guesthouse or an easy-care rented house that belongs to total strangers. But where should it be? Should you buy British or chase the sun?

The first difficulty with sunshine is the distance you have to travel to get it. The only way is to fly, but flying with children is not like flying alone. It isn't just a matter of buying yourself an expensive magazine and seeing how well you can control calf cramp in a confined space. Before you try anything more ambitious than the Glasgow Shuttle you should do some ground work.

For this exercise you will need two children with very small bladders and even smaller boredom thresholds. Next find a single-decker bus that will take you on a journey of at least one hour and choose a time of day when there will only be room for everyone to sit in their seat and stay there.

How was it? Admittedly you won't have had a lipsticky stewardess plying you with chicken salad and lemon-scented hand wipes, at least not if you were travelling where I live. And, likely as not, there weren't any in-transit videos or brown paper sickbags to play with. But, in other respects, it should have been a lot easier than the run from Gatwick to Malaga. There was very little risk of being hijacked, less still of plummeting 30,000 feet to certain destruction *and*, if things got really bad, you had the option of getting off at the next stop and phoning for a cab.

Do you really want to do it for three or four hours? With all the worries of whether to buy your duty-frees on the way out or on the way home, and did you turn the gas off?

And, when you get there, to this place in the sun, what are you going to do? Between breakfast time and afternoon tea you won't be able to let your children leave the shade of a very large parasol. You'll have to tie sunhats on them and baste them regularly in sunscreen. Why not go somewhere cooler?

You probably know as many people as I do who swear their children like nothing better than two weeks in a remote French gîte, drinking watered generic red and hiking five kilometres every morning to buy a couple of baguettes from a sour-faced old biddy in a black frock. They are all liars. Small British children do not like this sort of carry-on. They do not like food that has to be dragged from its shell waving a white flag. Nor are they too wild about olive groves, ice-cream that gives you amoebic dysentery or statues of men with bare bottoms. It's a funny thing about statues. In a town near me there's a beauty of John Hampden pointing the way to Westminster with the restrained use of one finger. People trudge past him every day laden with Eurosize Daz and never give him a glance. But, if someone moved him to Barcelona, they'd photograph him, examine him until they had a crick in their neck and bring home small souvenir replicas of him set in acrylic.

We were talking about children and the places you shouldn't take them. I'll tell you what children really like. They like Norfolk. They like it best in a very small caravan, but you should not give in to their every whim. I'll tell you why they like Norfolk. The roundabouts are small and slow. You are never far from a chip shop. It never gets so hot that your mother gets vicious with your sunhat. And it has empty beaches where you can throw sand and go Wheeeeeeh to your heart's content. It has everything a child could ask for but it has had such a bad press that you will ignore my advice and go somewhere fancy. Like Brighton.

Now I'm not here to condemn Brighton. Its tawdry splendour has a place in my adult heart, despite what it has done to me. There are places there that will feed you on foreign food, top up your glass and let you linger over the free cabaret, even on a Sunday. There's a beach where you can take off all your clothes and recover through sleep. And there is always something to look at. But you can't make sandcastles in Brighton. And those pebbles are murder to walk on. You must remember how important sand is to small children. And not any old sand. That fine, white stuff so prized by travel books may make a superb backdrop for your batik sarong but it is useless for building Conway Castle. And that essentially is all children want to do at the seaside.

If you start to look restless they may agree to a quick round of clock golf, but what they prefer is to get straight down there as soon as breakfast is done and set their stalls out. One bucket and spade per head is the least you can get away with, and, if your resources run to a fistful of those little paper flags, so much the better. You can also buy shaped moulds such as you might use for jellies, but I wouldn't bother. Those in the know tell me that, when it comes to recreating *Ark Royal* or burying a hundred and sixty pounds of windburned middle-management, buckets is best.

You'll also need sunoil, three times as many towels as you would

think possible, ten times as much food and raincoats. A hurricane lamp is a good idea as well. Normal children refuse to leave the beach until the last ray of daylight has died. If one of yours agrees to go shopping for postcards in the middle of the day, he is sickening for something.

All this makes for a long day. Sensible adults do it in shifts. After all, it is your holiday too. One of you must stay sober enough to deal with those who try to abscond, drown or slice off their big toe, but whoever's turn it is to be the other one *should* be able to snuggle down in his Arctic sleeping bag with a good book and a whimsical little Bag-in-a-Box from Oddbins. The book must not be too good though. This is not the time to be tackling *Anna Karenina*, because, even though you're the one with the Position Closed sign hanging round your neck, every three lines someone will want to tell you that they just seed Jaws and can you take them to the toilet.

If it's your turn on duty, there are stacks of whizzo things you can do to pass the time. Bury your own legs in the sand. Wonder what's happening at Old Trafford. Wish you'd worn something warmer. And each hour make several trips to the toilets because your children prefer a stinking insanitary urinal with a broken handdrier to piddling in the sea.

Have you ever thought of a holiday camp? No, please don't dismiss it out of hand. Let me tell you about them first. You'll have heard a lot of biased stories about them being full of tattooed *Sun* readers and brassy women with midriff bulge. About the draughty billets, the scumbag cabaret and how everything is awash in brown ale.

All of this is perfectly true.

Children of nine and older enjoy themselves so much at these places that you won't see them all week. There are activities for all weathers and abilities, and you won't have to sink your hand in your pocket every time they want to move on to something new. They'll also like the food. It's the sort of mass-produced bilge that has to be zapped with ketchup and swallowed fast. Only children and those who smoke sixty Park Drive a day would dream of saying it tasted all right.

But if you are the sort of adult who likes a quiet time with a new Ruth Rendell and a box of Milk Tray, a holiday camp is not for you. Isn't there someone you could pay to take your children for you? You don't all have to spend your holidays together, and if your children look like they're developing into the sort of people who'll put their names down for Miss Lovely Legs you should start thinking seriously about taking separate holidays. There are many ways of achieving this, and some are cheaper than others.

One is to hire a nanny with letters after her name and leave her in charge while you go to Venice on the Orient Express. You can give your children the feeling that they're getting a holiday too by authorising iced lollies *ad libitum* and letting them all stand down from room-cleaning. This does not come cheap. Apart from the nanny's wages and the iced lollies there will be the basic cost of your holiday, a complete new wardrobe, because everything you own will be stained with Airfix glue, and later on a phone bill with some hefty international collect-call charges. But, when you get back, you'll feel you've really had a holiday. The children will greet you warmly, the nanny will have got the tangles out of their hair, and your dog will be so joyful that you haven't run away and left him after all that he will flatten you and your bag full of Venetian glass before you set foot in the house.

Another method is to send the children away while you stay at home. School trips are a good bet. Amongst all those familiar people he'll be so busy pairing off and switching allegiances and bunks that he won't have time to get homesick. The hardest part will be getting him ready to go. Everything, even his pyjama cord, will have to be marked with his name, and there will be something on the list of essential equipment, like Sensible Shoes, that will make him turn very cussed in the Co-Op Sensible Shoe Department. But, when he comes back, he'll be full of useful information on how glass is made, what it costs to keep a lifeboat afloat, and what Mrs Robinson wears in bed.

If the school isn't running anything, another organisation your children belong to might be: like the Brownies or the Red Cross. A couple of weeks mucking in and tittering till dawn without you telling them to go to sleep will do you all a lot of good. And, if it comes to it and there's nothing convenient you can put them down for, you'll just have to blot the tears off your chequebook and send them on an activity holiday.

The best of these are great. Pricey. But great. I wish someone would send me on one. I'm talking about the ones staffed by qualified instructors, where they are as interested in getting the children into the cricket nets or improving their yo-yo technique as they are in taking your money. There are places where whole families can go and do their own things. Once your children have had their fill of digging deep holes in beaches, one of these can be a very wise move. You need only meet up at mealtimes, and the locations are often superb. Country seats and public schools with plenty of space to go for long, thinking mooches while others tap dance and screen paint.

There are farms, as well, that can offer you relief from enforced togetherness. Farms where you can stay while your children are allowed to collect the eggs and slow up the day's work with questions. These places usually have a pony that will let people sit on it, a gate that may be swung on, and a highly intelligent black and white dog who whips in any stragglers and keeps them from wandering. I can't understand how any farmer can be bothered with hey-nonnies from Highgate who scoff three poached eggs, read the *Observer* from cover to cover and reckon they've had a pretty hard day, but thankfully lots of them do. Make sure you are going to that sort of farm, though. Some of them aren't. Some of them are bed and breakfast in a place where pig space is calculated to the Eurodollar per square centimetre. In which case I'd rather stay home.

Staying at home does not have to mean staying at home. You can go out for day trips, and, if you have a car, you don't even have to book it in advance. You can get up, take a look at the weather and then ask, 'Where shall we go?'

Be very careful not to add, 'Anywhere you like.' I've seen strong men brought down by reckless generosity. In fact, if there's somewhere you definitely don't want to go you should say so at once: 'Apart from Billing Aquadrome, where would you like to go?' You'll be surprised at how modest children's ideas tend to be. They won't want to do anything that means four hours sucking barley sugar in the back of the car with their parents not speaking.

But you may have something special in mind. Like moving forwards very slowly in a queue outside Madame Tussauds. Adults have this perverse habit of wanting to be wherever they are not. They pay for a patch of almost-green-belt and immediately start wondering whether anyone's doing any interesting street theatre in Covent Garden. And the nearer they live to Coventry, the more they long for the taste of salt on their lips. This is the source of an ancient Midlands tradition called A Run To The Coast. No matter where you live you cannot possibly be further from the sea than I am, and what I don't know about Runs to the Coast is not worth knowing.

You start the day before with the early evening weather forecast. On the basis of a flimsy promise that it *may* snow in Dorset you must make your decision. If you get the green light, you must then cut a lot of sandwiches, stick them in the fridge and get to bed early. The die is then cast.

You must all be up at first light, cozzies in the bag, flasks filled and ready to scramble. Either you make a dash for it, hoping they'll all sleep until you park next to the Esplanade Deckchair Kiosk just after eight, or you take the whole journey at a steadier pace and stop at a Happy Eater for breakfast and your first row.

When you get to the seaside, it may not look as nice as you'd remembered it. Most of the fishing smacks and gnarled old salts have been replaced by plastic forks and polystyrene chip trays, and you would not believe how early the Bingo starts up. But you've travelled a long way, so you may as well enjoy yourselves.

Get down on to the beach before the boarding houses release their first breakfast sitting. These people book a week at Bella Vista and think they own the place. By ten o'clock they are everywhere, with their windbreaks and their frisbees, and they are reluctant to allow day-trippers the space for even one small, sandy towel.

Once you have a place on the beach, don't leave it unattended for a moment. Each time you remember something you've left in the car, send one member of the family back for it, while the rest of you sit tight. At about five o'clock it will suddenly go very chilly and the boarders will start to head back to Bella Vista, leaving you alone with the sea, the sky and several thousand Cornetto wrappers.

This is the toughest part of the day. Your children will not want to come away and you won't want to face the M25. Each child will have a bucket full of things he cannot possibly leave behind. Dozens of identical shells. Putrefying crab's claws. Sachets of sugar from the beach café. And you will have sand everywhere.

Here is what to do. First of all, be a good sport about the cold and the failing light and let them have another half hour. After all, we're a long while dead, and at least you can be thankful that you'll be sleeping in your own bed before the night is out. And you will not have had to earn your rest by surviving Whistling Jimmy Reilly and the Caister Organolians in the Pier End Summer Spectacular. Spare a thought for the poor souls at Bella Vista.

When you've played extra time, get them back to the car and make them put their jimjams on. Don't worry about breaking down on the motorway. Nothing brings sympathy and practical help faster than the sight of pyjama'd children many miles from home.

Next, buy them some very hot, salty chips and a bottle of Tizer. Then, as soon as they've swallowed the last chip, make them all go to the lavatory, even the ones who only just went. Now you must drive like the clappers. One by one they'll tell you they feel sick. Don't stop. If you do, they'll stop feeling it and actually be it. Instead, wind the windows down and sing 'Ten Green Bottles' until they've gone back to sleep. I regret to say that on some of our more ambitious trips we have turned in desperation to the 'Twelve Days of Christmas', which is probably why nothing will induce me to sing it come December, and I'm not all that struck with Runs to the Coast.

What your children might like to do for a day out is go to the swings. Just the local ones. And they'd like it even more if you let them take a ball, the dolls' prams, the laser guns and a big bag of jelly babies. This may not be your idea of a holiday but Monte Carlo will still be there when this part of your life has passed.

Or they might like to go to a cinema to see something very frightening. Or to an airport, if you can find one where they still let you watch planes take off and land. You might even tempt them with a museum, as long as it's not a big one and as long as there's a museum shop where you can buy postcards of dinosaurs. For some time my family's favourite outing was to tramp around a builder's furnished Show House, opening all the kitchen cupboards and deciding which bedrooms they'd like to have. It was pretty peeving for the women in the sales office who were there with their padded shoulders to talk to serious buyers, but who cares. They were hard women and so was I. We don't often do it these days. Mostly we head for somewhere big and open where they can all run free and go Neeeeeeeow as much as they want, because that's what they like best. Apart from Norfolk.

I don't know whether you've noticed, but the days of children being seen and not heard are over. They went out with ration books and the Glenn Miller Band. Children today are sophisticated, shock-proof and very vocal. If you want to take up talking to children, you'll have no difficulty getting started.

When they are very young, children like rambling chats with patient adults. A conversation with a four year old can cover an amazing amount of ground in a short space of time. 'Why have you come to see my Mummy? My Daddy's got a blue car. My Mummy's gone to the toilet. Why has she? We've got a red kettle. Why have you got a nasty spot on your nose?'

As a parent, you must remember that encounters like this have limited appeal to people who don't love your children. You mustn't keep slipping out of the room to check on the Crown Roast, leaving people stranded with your toddler. You'll make them nervous. You may be able to field his questions with ease, but they may not. Why should they? They may not be able to understand a blind word he says.

Personally, I never try to talk to other people's children. Good manners prevent me from saying things like 'Get down from there at once!' or 'Stop that immediately, you hateful wretch!' so I find it safer to remain silent. There is always the danger that, if one sounds the tiniest bit friendly, they may stagger across and wipe their top lip on one's coat.

As your own children get older, teach them to say things like, 'Hello, I'm Harry and I'm just on my way out.' Please don't ask them to do their Frank Spencer impersonation. You are the only person who will be able to watch it without cringing. Likewise with telephones. Teach them to answer, and ask who's calling.

Teach them to write down messages *and* pass them on. But don't leave your three year old to have a long natter with an unidentified caller. It may be someone calling peaktime from Australia with a business offer. Someone who doesn't want to hear Harry sing 'Twinkle Twinkle, Little Star' across thousands of expensive miles.

It's you he should sing to. You he should spin his yarns to. And you he should turn to with those awkward questions.

There are some subjects children save for special moments. Inconvenient moments. Subjects like death.

Death is a great favourite for doctor's waiting rooms, the silent sitting rooms of elderly relations, and anywhere else where those for whom the call must soon come are gathered in numbers.

'Do little children ever die? Why is it mostly old people that die? Is the old lady sitting next to us going to die soon? How soon? Before teatime? Will she be able to come back? Not ever? Not ever ever ever? Can I have a Toffo?'

The things that interest children about death are the things that interest us all. What does it feel like? And what if you don't like it? If you are of a religious persuasion, you will have more answers to these questions than I have. The other aspects of death that fascinate children will probably have you in as much difficulty as they do me. What if they bury you and you're not really dead? What if they burn you and you still need your body? And how can Snowball be in heaven when her skellington is next to the raspberry canes? I can only advise you that children can take quite a lot of straight talk. It seems that, the nearer we get to our own deaths, the more we need it wrapped up.

Father Christmas can give you difficult moments, as well. You'll get away with barefaced lies for years, with your child hanging up his stripy sock and leaving a bucket of water for the reindeer. Then some nine year old cynic will come along and sow a seed of doubt in his mind, and questions will be asked. 'Is Father Christmas true? Swear it on my *Blue Peter Annual*? Ruth says it's Anthony

Merrick's grandad. How can he buy all those things? Does he have a garage for his sledge? What would happen if I was awake when he came? I bet Anthony Merrick gets all the best things.'

In case you hadn't guessed it, let me tell you that Father Christmas is a very difficult man to justify. For one thing, if the shops can start in mid-August, how come he has to leave everything until Christmas Eve? Then there are night storage heaters, wood-burning stoves and burglar alarms. How do you explain him getting past that lot? Is it worth the bother? Has the time come for you to tell the truth and let Harry stop at the Sixth Form Disco till midnight on Christmas Eve? If it's important to you to keep up the pretence, the only thing to do is hood your eyes mysteriously and put it all down to magic. You can adopt the same technique for the Tooth Fairy and the Easter Bunny.

There are a few things you can't put down to magic. Taboos that will be broken even though you would rather they were not. On some subjects, children will give you no quarter. One of them is sex.

Sex used to be something you learned about blindfolded in a school lavatory full of virgins. You all groped around in the dark until someone stumbled on an answer that sounded plausible. It was very much like playing Call My Bluff. Later on, quite a lot later on, someone else held up a card with the real answers on. Some of them were surprising. And some of them weren't.

Nowadays it's on the curriculum, and Mrs Robinson sees to a lot of it. There are information packs, discussion groups and real-life, throbbing biology captured on video tape. And, although no one seems very much the wiser, young people today are certainly ignorant in a much more relaxed, wide-ranging way than they were thirty years ago. I'd guess school toilets aren't as much fun as they used to be, though.

The very young have no conscious interest in sex at all. You can get some beautiful books that explain to a toddler how a new baby is growing inside Mummy, but he would prefer you to read him something less improbable, like 'The Old Woman and the Vinegar

Bottle'. A new baby growing inside Mummy? And then popping out through a little doorway? Come on! Do you think he was born yesterday! He's been around a bit, you know! Seen a few of these babies. Great, big, lumpen creatures in pompom hats. Do you seriously expect him to believe that that's what's going on under your dungarees? Okay, okay, how did it get there? A little seed with a tail swam all the way until he found an egg? Sure he did! Maybe you should go and have another lie-down. And that little doorway? Is it doubleglazed? Does it have a mailbox? Or a lock? On the outside? Frankly, he would rather play with his Lego than listen to rubbish like this. If you insist on telling him something, try the one about the stork and the gooseberry bush. At least that won't give him nightmares about a redfaced hulk with a rusk in its hand crawling out from under his mum's frock and kicking the door shut behind it.

When he gets older, you can try the authorised version, but I do mean older. Expect no more than the odd question, the odd, very odd question, until about nine. For years I held ante-natal classes in my own home. My teaching aids were always lying around: foam-rubber reconstructions of intimate organs. One thing attracted my children particularly. It was a book of photographs of lifelike models of the baby's journey into the outside world. They pored over it so often I'd have said there was nothing those children didn't know about childbirth. But I found out later it was the baby they liked. He had a squidged up face and wrinkly little fingers and they thought he was lovely. They hadn't paid much attention to anything else.

Any questions you are asked will require very simple answers. Don't dive off to find your textbooks and a sharp pencil for explanatory diagrams. By the time you get back he'll have wandered off to hold his sisters' skipping rope and have forgotten what it was he had asked you. Distil your answer into a single sentence. If he wants to know more he'll come back with a supplementary. But not necessarily straight away. Children like to leave their supplementaries on a low burner for a while to allow the

whole episode to pass from your mind. You'll be on a standing-room only Bank Holiday train, trying not to faint, and he'll come over loud and clear with something that's been on his mind. 'And what exactly *does* wanking mean?'

If he's going to be interested at all, it will be in the visible signs of sex. If you give him the opportunity, he will notice that your body isn't quite the same as his. He may decide the most tactful thing is not to mention it, but he may not have that much self-control. Whatever you do, don't run away with the idea that he in any way envies you. If he enquires politely about your pubic hair, don't sit him down and tell him he'll have some himself before too much longer. He will be appalled. Who the hell wants to have to tuck that lot down the front of their strides before they can go out and play

Blake's Seven? Why couldn't you have had some worthwhile peculiarity for him to inherit? Like being able to fly. And what other nasty genetic flukes have you got up your sleeve? Bad breath? The need to sleep every Sunday afternoon? Or hairy nostrils and a really depressing mortgage? A child can be severely traumatised by the thought of having to spend money on razor blades and tampons, and all to end up looking like you.

Better, I think, not to be too thorough too early. With money so short in schools, it can only be a matter of time before luxuries like Sex Education are dropped. If they want to, our children can pick it

up and take it back to the traditional forum for hairstyling, speculation, and sexual bravado, the Bog. And I should think no one will be more relieved than Mrs Robinson.

While we're on the subject, there are other things children do in the toilet. Here are some of them. Forget to use the flush. Forget what they have gone there for but stay there anyway singing loudly and tunelessly while a queue of desperate people forms outside the door. Use all the paper. Use no paper whatsoever. Get there too late.

Let's start at the beginning. For the first two years of his life you will catch whatever he does in a nappy. If it lands anywhere else you should put it down to luck, good or bad. You *can* sit him on a potty when he's a week old but you are as likely to catch a cold as you are to catch anything of substance.

It is all very simple. Until he's about two years old he will be physically incapable of co-ordinated control. That is the truth. If anything could have speeded up my escape from grey terry towelling and an ominously stagnant bucketful every morning, I would have found it. You will just have to be patient.

When he's two, go out and buy a pot, two dozen pairs of knickers, a sponge for the puddles, and a large bag of treacle toffees. The toffees are for keeping your mouth busy when you might otherwise feel like saying something. Sometimes it helps if you let him choose the potty himself. Then he can't refuse to sit on it on the grounds that he finds green so inhibiting. Make sure he chooses a simple bum-shaped receptacle. There is no need for safety straps, musical accompaniment, or a hand that shoots out with a square of Andrex and a certificate of merit.

If there is going to be a new baby arriving in the near future, leave the pot until family life has returned to normal. There is no hurry, and the later you leave it, the faster he'll learn.

Two year olds have pretty strong views on potties. When you introduce him to it he will either run away and hide or he will spend the rest of the week sitting on it. There's no predicting. I can understand this. I feel pretty strongly about them myself. After years of seeing ours empty when it should have been full, full when it should have been empty, and never ever where it should have been when we needed it in a hurry, I'm bound to. The day we stopped needing it, I danced a samba with the man at the Household Waste Tip.

If Harry objects strongly to it, leave it alone for a while. He'll either warm to the idea of doing something different or turn out to be one of those people who'd rather wait until their legs are a bit longer and then use the lavatory. He may find it a bit degrading, being debagged by a running tackle and made to sit in front of those *Playschool* presenters until he's got a red ring round his backside. He may prefer to go off somewhere private and see to things for himself. And then carry it back, lapping at the brim, for you to inspect and admire. Whatever his attitude, he won't want to be bothered with it if he's in the middle of something interesting. That's when you'll need the sponge and the toffees.

In the summer, it's not so bad because you can fling the windows open and have all those knickers dry by next morning. But, in the winter, it's grim. The earth is damp, the air is damp, and suddenly your sculptured broadloom has gone the same way. Will the sun ever shine again? Will you ever get rid of that smell? And is this child stupid or just plain wicked?

For the first few days of pottying you'll find it easier to stay at home. Make sure you've got plenty of bread in, introduce Harry to the concept of bladder control, and then curl up in an armchair with a good book.

Eventually you will have to make a dash for it. The bread will run out, the library will send you a reminder that your books are overdue, and you, Harry and Harry's bladder will have to face the world. What do you do? Put your coat on, wring him out hard and then run? Plan your trip with the help of an Ordnance Survey map and an up-to-date list of public lavatories? Or put him back in a nappy and tell him to hang loose? You could do. It might confuse him, though.

I went out and got one of those organiser bags with lots of

pockets and compartments. Other people might use them for their cordless hairstyler and their *Cosmopolitan* Five Year Assertiveness Planner, but not me. I had a pocket for dry knickers, a pocket for wet knickers and a big one for the toffees. We went all over the place, me and my bag. And we learned quite a lot. We learned that dresses are easier than trousers, and that dungarees worn with an anorak and buckled shoes are very difficult indeed. We learned that department stores have their lavatories on the top floor; that Mothercare just don't have any; and that airport facilities are really for bona fide passengers and that if you are a bona fide needy woman with a wet Harry, waiting for a bona fide travelling granny, you may well have to get on bended knee before anyone will let you in.

You should be careful on your travels not to mix up the compartment for dry knickers with the one for wets and to carry a large strong polythene bag for the ones that defy description.

When you set off on your journey, don't make the mistake of asking him every one hundred yards whether he wants to. If you keep pestering him, he will either say Yes to shut you up and have you struggling with those dungarees for a teaspoonful, or he will say No on principle. The only times I can tell you he definitely will want to go are on that long stretch of the Piccadilly Line between Knightsbridge and South Kensington or just before a photo finish in the Coronation Cup.

All other things being equal, if Harry is a girl you are likely to be finished with nappies sooner than if Harry is a boy. Especially at night. And that's a funny thing because it's women who have the reputation for small, weak bladders. A boy who can't make it through the night when he's six or seven years old is not unusual. You can choose between changing his sheet every morning, or giving him a fireman's lift to the bathroom in the middle of the night and telling him where he is. Talk quietly and reassuringly to him until he wakes up enough to understand. Don't yell at him, unless he does something really despicable. Yes, I'd say doing it on your feet was despicable enough.

This lavatorial interlude brings me back to talking to children, and what you tell them on the day you do Naming of Parts. Years ago male bits always had funny names because they looked funny, and female bits didn't have names at all because they were invisible. Then someone discovered Carnaby Street and the clitoris and things really took off. For many parents this was the signal to start teaching their children the proper words and get the whole business out in the open. But it didn't work. Because teaching children the right words doesn't give them the other thing they need – a finely tuned sense of when it's all right to use them. And are we sure we want it all out in the open anyway?

There are still people around who can remember when the sun never set on British soil, and some of them may be sitting in rocking chairs within earshot of your children. Testicles would not have gone down well with Queen Mary and, though I'm no prude, I can do without them myself. And I feel unable to insist that my daughters use the right words for the bits you can only see with a torch and a dentist's mirror. It takes at least three brandies to get anything gynaecological past my lips.

I have found from experience that when it comes to talking to children there are three things you should try to bear in mind. One is that anything below the belt and above the knee can be covered quite nicely by judicious use of the word Bum. The second is that children are always willing to shelve anything controversial, delicate or disgusting until a more inconvenient moment. And the third and most important is that there is nothing better for rooting out your prejudices and shaking your foundations than listening to a child and realising that he has seen, clearly and freshly, something you were too old to have noticed.

Index